CW00674200

The Colours of Scottish Cities

Alan Millar

Image work by Michael Eyre

Capital Transport

Acknowledgements

While enjoying the memories evoked by the pictures that follow, offer up your appreciation of the enthusiasm that drove their photographers to capture images of their everyday that are the bygone and history of today; and for their generosity and foresight in making them available for publications like this – in particular Roy Marshall, Geoffrey Morant, Jim Thomson, Bill Philip, Ian Maclean and Iain MacGregor. Special thanks also to Gavin Booth and Bob McGillivray for their assistance with the sections on their home cities of Edinburgh and Aberdeen and to Steven Pirie for providing access to the photographs taken by the late Bill Philip.

Also be hugely appreciative – as I am – of Jim Whiting of Capital Transport for providing the medium to publish them, of the Omnibus Society and the Online Transport Archive for access to the photographs in their extensive image archives, and for the skills, patience, standards of perfection and unbridled enthusiasm of Mike Eyre for the work he has done to restore to original condition and colours those films upon which time and atmosphere has been less forgiving.

We have tried to ensure that each image is correctly attributed – our apologies to anyone whose picture is wrongly named.

Front cover Princes Street, the main thoroughfare in Scotland's capital city of Edinburgh, and a cross-section of the municipal fleet operating in the early 1970s. Metro-Cammell Orion-bodied Leyland Titan PD2/20 500 (LFS 500) was the last of 100 new in 1954 for tram replacement and one of 300 delivered by 1957. A 1972 Leyland Atlantean AN68/1R with Alexander AL body is close behind, with a 1960 Weymann-bodied Leyland Tiger Cub to its rear. *Gavin Booth*

Back cover Glasgow operated locally-built Albion Venturers until 1963 when the newest examples, like B114 (FYS 496), were 10 years old. They had Weymann bodies and 8ft-wide CX37SW chassis. *Geoffrey Morant*

Rear cover Aberdeen 191 (HRG 191) was one of 45 Crossley-bodied Daimler CVG6s new in 1954/55. *Geoffrey Morant*

First published 2016

ISBN 978-1-85414-401-0

Published by Capital Transport Publishing Ltd
www.capitaltransport.com

Printed in the EU

Contents

Introduction 4

Glasgow 6

Edinburgh 46

Aberdeen 74

Dundee 98

The Companies 118

The Independents 132

Introduction

Above Glasgow L221 (SGD 123), an Alexander-bodied Leyland Titan PD2/24 new in 1959. *Geoffrey Morant*

Colours must surely lie behind much of our fascination with buses, especially of the era before privatisation and consolidation of the operating industry replaced many local identities with national ones.

That certainly is true of the Scottish cities, which like local authorities across the UK painted a unique identity on the municipal bus fleets that they owned. Those distinctively coloured buses were very much part of the urban fabric that they served, reinforcing civic pride.

As a pre-school child in Glasgow in the 1950s, I have no doubt that the colours of the city's trams and buses – bright green, cream and orange against soot-blackened buildings and often under rain-depositing clouds – helped draw my attention to their existence, along with their different shapes and tuneful sounds.

The climate may have been drier on the east coast, but the madder and white buses of Edinburgh and the different green-based colour schemes of Aberdeen and Dundee were just as effective in giving those cities a sense of place.

Mention of those four names makes it important to define that other part of this book's title: cities. Modern Scotland currently has seven thanks to jubilee and millennium moves to elevate more United Kingdom towns to city status. But here we look primarily at Glasgow, the largest city; Edinburgh, the capital; and the east coast ports of Aberdeen and Dundee, all of which operated their own municipal bus fleets until the 1970s.

Of the 'new' cities of Inverness, Stirling and Perth, only Perth – which regained city status in 2012 – operated municipal buses, which Alexander's took over in 1934. They continued to have a separate identity, as shown in the final section of the book, which looks at some of the colourful company buses in these five cities.

Not only did the 'big four' have substantial corporation bus operations, but they also clung on to and in three cases continued investing in their tram fleets into the immediate post-war period, Edinburgh and Dundee closing theirs in 1956, Aberdeen in 1958 and Glasgow – the last city tram operator in all Britain at the time – in September 1962.

Glasgow also was the only sustained Scottish operator of trolleybuses and the last place in the UK to introduce them, building up a large yet unloved system between 1949 and 1958, running it down from 1959 to May 1967. At its peak of 194 vehicles, this was the third largest trolleybus fleet after the large London Transport one and Belfast's, yet its patchy penetration of the city meant that many residents were oblivious to its existence.

On the other hand, they had a better chance of knowing about trolleybuses than their counterparts in Dundee, where two operated from September 1912 until May 1914, abandoned

Below left Edinburgh 293 (WFS 293K), an Alexander-bodied Leyland Atlantean PDR1A/1, on the city's Royal Mile. *Omnibus Society/Roy Marshall*

Below right Glasgow trolleybus TB14 (FYS 714), a BUT 9641T with Metro-Cammell body to London Transport Q1 standard dating from the start of operations in 1949. Photographed on 10th May 1964. *Tony Belton*

not on account of their traction but because the poorly surfaced out-of-town route they served would have made any contemporary bus unpleasant.

Keeping trams for as long as they did added to the variety of the four cities' bus fleets, for they followed the immediate post-war boom in fleet replacement of worn-out buses with a second to replace the trams. In Edinburgh and Dundee that included – in very different ways – the acquisition of second-hand London double-deckers.

These also were the years when Alexander's coach-building business transformed itself from the in-house department of the Scottish Motor Traction group into an independent company with an ever-wider customer base and, from 1958, a large new factory in Falkirk. All four cities entered the post-war era sourcing most of their bodywork from a variety of bodybuilders, especially from the Metro-Cammell Weymann sales organisation's factories in Birmingham and Surrey. Steadily Alexander's accounted for an increasing proportion of their orders, virtually all of them from 1962 onwards.

These fleets were far from immune to the negative pressures hitting public transport across the UK from the mid-1950s as car ownership grew and lifestyle changes diminished some of the demand for travel. Consequently, the drive to contain rising operating costs and falling revenue saw the cities simplifying – or attempting to simplify – their bus liveries.

Spray painting encouraged them to apply fewer colours over greater areas of bodywork, while reducing such detail embellishments as gold or black lining and separately coloured roofs. These also were the years when commercial advertising was either introduced for the first time or expanded in scope. Two of the cities also joined the brief – but happily short-lived – trend of leaving most bodywork in the unappealing 'colour' of bare metal.

Today, Edinburgh's buses – still in municipal ownership of the arm's length Lothian Buses – carry a distinct identity, one that plays due homage to decades of tradition. In Dundee, National Express had painted the city's buses in the same colour as those in Birmingham and the Black Country but in 2015 rebranded them as Xplore Dundee with a two-tone green influenced by the corporation's livery of the early 1970s.

The Glasgow and Aberdeen undertakings are subsumed into First's national identity, in the former case along with the remnants of many of the differently coloured company fleets that once served the city.

If reading the text through the eyes of someone raised outside Scotland, please excuse a couple of colloquialisms. 'Stance' is Scottish for 'stand' as in 'bus stand', and 'housing schemes' are 'housing estates' when built by or for public authorities.

Above Aberdeen 315 (URG 315), a 1963 Alexander-bodied Daimler CVG6, in its original livery. *Omnibus Society/Roy Marshall*

Below left Glasgow was Alexander's launch customer for a new design of body for Leyland Atlanteans delivered from 1962 onwards and converted for one-man operation from 1969. This is Knightswood Garage in June 1973, with LA83 (SGD 661) alongside newer LA440 and LA436. *Omnibus Society/Roy Marshall*

Below right Alexander (Northern) NPA173 (CWG 275), a 1950 Alexander-bodied Leyland Tiger PS1, leaving Aberdeen for Durris. *Geoffrey Morant*

Glasgow

Scotland's largest city, the west coast port of Glasgow, was the last to introduce corporation buses and the last – in the British Isles as well as Scotland – to replace trams. Even so, by 1963 – the year after the trams went – it operated by some margin the largest bus fleet north of the border with over 1,500 motorbuses and trolleybuses on its books.

There long was a sense that the buses were the poorer relation of the municipal transport department, their drivers and conductors perched below their tram colleagues in the pecking order and their routes serving less important city centre streets until the trams disappeared in 1957-62. If the motorbuses enjoyed less exalted status, the trolleybuses were the poorest cousins of all, introduced in 1949-58 largely through the enthusiasm of one prominent local politician, but neglected after his death and scrapped within five years of the trams.

Yet Glasgow's buses really were important to the city and in common with the trams were arguably the most colourful in Scotland: green, cream and orange, the orange later giving way to various shades of yellow as spray painting was introduced. The distribution of colours differed on trolleybuses, largely for practical reasons.

It is convenient to say that the colours reflected the city's tribal religious divide, Protestant orange and Irish Catholic green, but their origins were far less controversial.

From the start of municipal operation in 1894, tram routes were identified by five colours applied to the upper deck panels: white and deep shades of red, blue, green or yellow. In the days of horse traction, the lower panels were cadmium and cream. Electrification at the turn of the century demanded warning that these vehicles could move quickly without an animal attached.

Some American electric streetcars were painted orange and as a safety warning Glasgow adopted a similar shade – 'electric orange' – in place of cadmium on the lower panels, for much the same reason as British Rail trains gained yellow ends in the 1960s.

Buses never had route colours, their upper panels being painted a lighter, more yellowy green than the green route trams. Within Glasgow Corporation Transport, this was 'bus green' and it also went on the trams when service numbers replaced route colours from the late-1930s. Service numbers, incidentally, that duplicated many of those on the buses. It says much for the street wisdom of post-1938 Glaswegians that even along a lengthy stretch of streets through the East End and into the city centre served by quite different bus and tram routes both numbered 1, regulars could easily tell a bus apart from a tram.

GCT's first 14 buses – seven pairs of single-deckers from competing chassis manufacturers – were introduced in December 1924 on a route that complemented the extensive tram network

Glasgow was the last UK city to operate double-deck trams and the last to introduce trolleybuses. Until the trams went in September 1962, a short stretch of London Road at Bridgeton Cross also was the last place in the British Isles where trams, trolleybuses and motorbuses ran together. Crossley-bodied BUT 9613T trolleybus TB49 (FYS 810) new in 1958, is heading north-eastwards on route 106 while Coronation tram 1182, new in 1938, heads east on service 9 to Auchenshuggle. An Alexander-bodied Leyland PD2/20 of Central SMT is overtaking the trolleybus. *Paul Creswell*

to such an extent that it literally went out of its way to avoid streets with trams between Glasgow Green and the West End.

Early routes that followed it were short suburban feeders connecting with frequent trams but by the end of the 1920s – with low-frame 50-seat double-deckers arriving in quantity – buses came into their own, connecting new low density municipal and private housing on lengthy, mainly cross-city routes.

From 1930, municipal buses and trams were protected by a private act of parliament preventing company buses from carrying local passengers within the then city boundaries. That protection was diluted after postwar housing was built within new boundaries established in 1938 but it was 1982 – beyond the scope of this book – before the restrictions were lifted.

After 1963, all new buses were Alexander-bodied Leylands, but before then they were far more varied than the trams, which were designed by the transport department and with a few exceptions also built by its direct labour force. AEC, Leyland and locally-built Albion dominated prewar purchases, 19 Guy and 69 Daimler utilities were allocated in wartime, while AEC, Albion and Daimler were the immediate postwar favourites, Leyland returning to favour and ultimate dominance after it acquired Albion in 1951. From the late-1930s to mid-1950s most bodies came from factories in England.

Two other features helped distinguish Glasgow Corporation's postwar buses. One was an alphanumeric fleet numbering system, similar to Liverpool's. The other was the allocation of two complete sets of registration numbers for buses and ancillary vehicles, FYS 1-999 from 1947, SGD 1-999 from 1957, though SGD 741 to 949 were never taken up following the introduction of year suffix identifiers, in Glasgow's case from 1964.

If fleet and registration numbers ever came near to matching one another, it was usually by accident. They were close on 145 AEC Regent IIIs, 20 Daimler CVD6s and the first 34 trolleybuses, but on 150 later Leylands they were tantalisingly out by just two and by 102 on another 100. That may have frustrated enthusiasts but for GCT there was no need. It recorded all data and filed registration documents in fleet number order, so the number plates were just a legal formality.

GCT's operations – buses and the circular Subway railway – transferred to the Greater Glasgow Passenger Transport Executive on 1 June 1973.

A208 (FYS 391), a Weymann-bodied AEC Regent III new in 1951 and still painted in its original livery, climbing Cathedral Street in 1962 away from the city centre, with part of the Glasgow Central College nearing completion behind. *Omnibus Society/Roy Marshall*

Pre-war vehicles

Postwar rebodying prolonged the lives of 128 prewar and wartime double-deckers. Oldest of these, withdrawn by 1957, were 23 Leyland Titan TD4s out of a batch of 60 dating from 1935, some if not all of which had torque converter transmission when new. These 23 all had manual gearboxes by the time they were rebodied. Walter Alexander & Company (Coachbuilders) Ltd, newly separated from its bus operating namesake following nationalisation of the Scottish Motor Traction group's bus companies, built their 52-seat Leyland-style bodies in 1949. There were no postwar Leylands in 1949 and these became plain and simple L1-23 in the alphanumeric series. The buses here are L3 (YS 2023) and L17 (YS 2059) lined up at the back of Knightswood Garage from where they departed for scrap in 1959. They are parked between Albion Venturers on the left and a rebodied pre-war AEC Regent on the right. *Jim Thomson*

Opposite All 45 of the new bodies for prewar Regents were ordered from Scottish companies. Ten came from Scottish Commercial Motor Company, the Crossley agent, which supplied a version of a body Crossley had built two years earlier on 50 new Regent IIIs. However, Scottish Commercial only assembled one of them, on Crossley frames, the other nine being built by Crossley using some parts from Scottish Commercial, with delivery extending into 1951. AR293 (BUS 185) became a driver trainer in April 1959, when this photograph was taken at Knightswood Cross a few stops west of the garage and driving school for the north of the city, with tram tracks still in use in the central reservation of this part of Great Western Road. It was cut down into a breakdown tender in December 1961 and survived in that form, repainted dark red, until sold for scrap in 1974. It was one of 100 buses delivered new in 1938 with highly appropriate BUS registrations. *John Kaye*

Alexander built new bodies on 15 out of 45 1937/38 manual gearbox AEC Regents selected for life extension in 1950. Like the 1935 Leylands, their original bodies from prolific prewar Glasgow coachbuilder F D Cowieson had proved less durable than contemporary Weymann products. With 265 postwar Regent IIIs in course of delivery, the rebodied examples were numbered AR266-310, though new Regent Vs delivered from 1955 included A266-310. This is AR307 (BGA 19) negotiating the complex five-way junction at Anniesland Cross on a summer evening before it was withdrawn from passenger service in September 1958. Had the bus preservation movement become established 10 years earlier than it did, it might still have been around today, for it survived until December 1958 as a driver trainer and saw five years' service in Berkshire with Reliance of Newbury. The bodies of these 15 buses were essentially to the same Leyland-influenced design as the TD4s, but with round-edged, rubber-mounted windows.
Jim Thomson

The AEC Regents

The most numerous and enduring of Glasgow's immediate postwar fleet were 265 AEC Regent IIIs new in 1948-51 with preselector gearboxes and air brakes, GCT having bought the only similarly equipped 'prewar' (new February 1940) RT-type Regent supplied outside London. Of these, 195 had all-metal bodies to a Metro-Cammell design with prewar styling origins. However, Metro-Cammell only bodied the first 95; the 100 delivered in 1951, including A262 (FYS 445) photographed at Drumoyne in the south-west of the city, came instead from Weymann, its still independent partner in the MCW sales organisation. It lasted in service until 1966, the year before the last Regent IIIs were withdrawn. *Jim Thomson*

With public transport use in decline, GCT made several economies in the presentation of its buses during the 1950s. Rear destination displays were removed, then intermediate 'via' points from the front. And in 1959 the livery was simplified to take advantage of the introduction of spray painting at its central works. The top half remained in the same shade of green, but various shades of orange and yellow were tried out on the bottom half before settling on yellow with a hint of orange. This is one of the more orange shades on A121 (FYS 221), a 1949 bus with Metro-Cammell body, between duties at Knightswood Garage. *Jim Thomson*

It did not need to happen but spray painting sometimes lacked subtlety, as evidenced by A134 (FYS 234), another of the 95 bodied by Metro-Cammell, on which mudguards and wings are yellow rather than black as on A121 in the previous picture. Happily, the painters masked the polished radiator before firing up their guns. *Jim Thomson*

The oldest of the postwar AECs – and arguably the most modern looking – were 50 with Crossley bodies built in 1948 and kept until 1964-66. This April 1960 view shows A62 (FYS 162) passing the municipal transport head office at 46 Bath Street, with its prominent clock on the corner of Renfield Street. Bath Street was one of the city centre thoroughfares on which tramlines were never laid. *John Kaye*

Twenty Regent IIIs had Northern Coachbuilders composite bodies, which proved less robust in service. A84 (FYS 184), photographed in June 1961 in the then 10-year-old corporation housing scheme at Priesthill, was new in early 1949 and was withdrawn in 1965. Only three survived until 1967, though these and 20 similar Daimlers survived largely unaltered in appearance. *Iain MacGregor*

Albions

The alphanumeric fleet numbering system introduced in 1947 began with makes identified by A, B, C and D prefixes. Besides A for AEC and D for Daimler, there was a solitary Crossley, C1 (which probably eluded colour photography throughout its 10 years in the fleet). Given that two types could not share the same letter, B was for Albion, which built its products within the city boundaries at Scotstoun on the north bank of the Clyde. It supplied 130 Venturer double-deckers between 1935 and 1942 and 138 more between 1947 and 1951, the last chassis arriving shortly before Leyland bought the company. The Albions were the most varied of all the double-deckers of this period, with seven different body styles from six coachbuilders. By Glasgow's postwar standards, the Venturer was obsolescent with a constant mesh manual gearbox demanding higher skills of drivers. There was little chance of that changing, as Albion saw its future with lorries rather than buses in 1947 and the following year declined to tender for a possible repeat order from Glasgow. The last came out of passenger service in 1963, although some survived longer as snowploughs. The upright profile of the Wakefield-built Charles Roberts bodies on B1-24, new in 1947/48, had a prewar look about them. B24 (EGA 30) and B17 (EGA 23) in this line-up of withdrawn Venturers at Knightswood came out of service in 1959 after just 11 years' use. To their immediate left are B40 (EGA 46) and B47 (EGA 53), new in 1949 with Metro-Cammell bodies, culled after 10 years. These two batches of 24 Venturers all were CX19 models with 9.1litre Albion engines.
Jim Thomson

The varying shades of orange and yellow lower panels are evident in this later scene from the Knightswood 'dump' where most buses awaited disposal. There were 24 with Metro-Cammell bodies virtually identical to the bodies on 195 AEC Regent IIIs. Hand-painted B31 (EGA 37) on the right saw 12 years' service before withdrawal in 1961, while B43 (EGA 49) in the orange version of spray-painted livery had come out of service the previous year. Sandwiched between them are two CX37S Venturers with 9.9litre engines. B53 (FYS 270) on the left was new in 1949 and was one of 40 with a four-bay Roberts body; it was unusual in being sold for further service, surviving until 1963 with Dunoon Motor Services on the Firth of Clyde. To its right is B89 (EGA 76), one of 10 bodied in Glasgow's East End in 1949 by Croft Bodybuilding & Engineering; another of the same batch, B92, has been preserved since withdrawal in 1963 and is displayed in Glasgow's Riverside transport museum. *Jim Thomson*

Roberts-bodied B52 (FYS 269) was among several vehicles partially repainted at Parkhead Garage, where the Albions were concentrated latterly. In common with most of these repaints, the bottom half was yellow with the 7in cream band above, while the top half remained untouched; there also was a version with top half repainted green and bottom half left orange with cream window surrounds. Following it is fully repainted B81 (FYS 298), with sun visors (or rain deflectors?) only above the opening windows. *Iain MacGregor*

This older Glasgow Albion, the former 786 (DGB 434), provides a link with the postwar fleet. With a long tradition of designing and building its trams, GCT also wanted to build its own bus bodies. It secured wartime permission in 1942 to assemble eight of these Metro-Cammell bodies to Weymann design on Venturer CX19 chassis in the bus works attached to Larkfield Garage. They came out of service between 1953 and 1956, and in 1955 two of them were sold to Dunoon Motor Services, which served the Clyde resort and neighbouring villages until 1965. *Omnibus Society/ Roy Marshall*

In 1946, GCT successfully sought parliamentary approval to build its own bus bodywork in peacetime and intended twice to use frames from the Metro-Cammell Weymann organisation as the basis of batches of 25 CX37S Venturers. Unable to pursue this within a suitable timescale, the first 25 were built instead by three West of Scotland bodybuilders and delivered in 1949/50. Besides the 10 built by Croft, there were 10 to Park Royal design by West Bromwich-based Brockhouse, which had opened a factory in Clydebank in 1948. This April 1960 view shows B99 (EGA 86), new 1950 and withdrawn 1961, in George Square on the busy 41 service from nearby Buchanan Street to the then new Easterhouse housing scheme on the city's eastern outskirts, a route begun three years earlier. A Scottish Omnibuses Bristol Lodekka is following behind. *John Kaye*

Scottish Aviation rode on the back of the postwar boom in demand for new buses by employing aircraft technology to build bodies using aluminium alloy instead of steel. Glasgow bought 20 of the only 21 double-deck bodies the Prestwick company built before quitting a market in which it sold many more single-deckers. Five of these were on Venturers, including B112 (EGA 99) new in January 1950. All five came out of service in 1961 and B112 lasted until the end of the following year as a driver trainer. *Iain MacGregor*

George Square in June 1959 and another Albion originally intended to have a GCT-built body. B114 (FYS 496) was the first of the only 8ft wide Venturers built for the UK. The 25 CX37SW chassis – offered originally for export markets – were delivered from nearby Scotstoun to Knightswood Garage with the intention that the transport department would soon assemble their bodies. That came to nothing and two years elapsed before Weymann bodied them in Surrey. One was written off in an accident in 1959 but most, B114 included, survived in passenger service until 1963. *Geoffrey Morant*

Only 10 years old when most were withdrawn in 1963, 22 of the 8ft wide Venturers were retained as snowploughs, clearing bus routes in harsh winter weather. As is all too evident from this photograph, tender loving care was off the agenda in this role for which some survived until 1966. By then, the private bus preservation movement was beginning to come together but a bid to buy one of these historic vehicles ultimately failed. *Campbell Sayers*

Thirty Venturer CX19s dating from 1939, 1940 and 1942 – all bodied by railway rolling stock and tram manufacturer R Y Pickering in Wishaw, Lanarkshire – were rebodied in 1952 by East Lancashire Coachbuilders at its Bridlington plant in East Yorkshire. These formed the new BR class and were among the last 'Brid-built' East Lancs buses, as the loss-making factory closed the following year. The chassis of BR27 (DGB 468), at Anniesland Cross, dated from 1940 and like most of the class was kept in service until 1960. When GCT justified its removal of intermediate destination blinds, one of its arguments was that they could confuse as much as they might inform. If this held any truth, the display on BR27 maybe bore out the claim. Cross-city service 6 did indeed service Duke Street, St Vincent Street and Crow Road but in that order only on westbound journeys. Eastbound from Garscadden to Provanmill, it has turned from Anniesland Road (where a red Central SMT Leyland is heading towards Clydebank) and will turn right into Crow Road; it will later reach St Vincent Street and then Duke Street. *Jim Thomson*

Daimlers

There were no Daimlers in the fleet until 25 Weymann-bodied COG6s arrived in late 1937 ready to strengthen services for the Empire Exhibition staged in Glasgow the following year. Wartime changed that, with 69 utility examples delivered in 1943-46, mostly CWA6s with AEC engines but also two CWG5s with Gardner 5LWs and five CWD6s in August 1945 with Daimler's own CD6. Immediate postwar purchases included another 109 Daimler-engined Daimlers, 108 of them CD6-powered CVD6s. Twenty arrived in 1949 with Northern Coachbuilders composite bodies similar to those on the 20 contemporary AEC Regent IIIs and afflicted by the same structural weaknesses (one example of each scrapped early and replaced by all-metal bodies from damaged chassis). Here D19 (FYS 119), in original livery with black lining out, stands ahead of spray-painted D20 on the forecourt of Larkfield Garage, its destination blind set for a football special. D19 went for scrap in 1965, D20 the previous year. *Jim Thomson*

Intermediate 'via' destination displays lasted long enough for D1 (FYS 101) to retain them immediately after repaint into the orange version of the spray-painted livery introduced in 1959. It has emerged into the evening sun from the Broomielaw terminus on the north bank of the Clyde underneath Glasgow Central railway station, a facility used from 1948 to 1963 for services to new council housing built on the Nether Pollok Estate. For entirely operational reasons, these routes minimised their exposure to traffic congestion by dropping their passengers on the edge of the city centre, leaving them to walk or use trams or other bus services to complete their journeys. D1 was withdrawn in 1964. *Jim Thomson*

Glasgow's first Alexander bodies to the steadily expanding coachbuilder's own design were built on 40 Daimler chassis. D51 (FYS 479), looking immaculate straight out of overhaul and parked opposite the Coplawhill tramcar works, was one of 49 CVD6s new in 1950. They were followed in 1951 by D60, with an 8ft wide version of the body on a CD650 chassis. There also was D66, a 7ft 6in CVD6 with 8ft Mann Egerton body. Neither the chassis of D60 nor the body of D66 lived up to their promise and in 1960 the bad parts were discarded and D66 returned to service with the body from D60 and survived in that form until 1965, the same year that D51 and other remaining exposed radiator CVD6s were withdrawn. *Phil Tatt/Online Transport*

D61-5, new in the summer of 1950, had Scottish Aviation bodies similar to Albions B109-13 and rebodied AECs AR276-85. This view of D63 (FYS 491) shows how the spray-painted livery was applied across mouldings intended originally for relief colour and black lining. It was operating from Possilpark Garage on service 8 linking the northern housing schemes at Milton and Balornock East with shops and major employers in Springburn, a route that did not penetrate the city centre. The *Glasgow Herald* billboard outside the shop addresses a seemingly perpetual question, 'Reforming the young delinquent'. *Campbell Sayers*

From tramway days, Glasgow was a double-deck city, with a few largely experimental exceptions operating single-deckers only where there was a physical restriction, even if passenger numbers did not justify so many seats. Its first postwar single-deckers were 43 Daimler CVD6s with dual door (forward entrance, rear exit) 33-seat bodies built in the Larkfield bus works on Metal Sections frames. Their styling, notably the three long window bays, was influenced by 100 'Cunarder' trams that GCT built at Coplawhill car works between 1948 and 1952. Construction of these 43 buses spread over that same period, with the first – DS43, numerically the last – entering service in September 1948. DS1-10 followed in June and December 1949, DS11-20 between March and August 1950, DS21-30 between January and September 1951, finally DS31-42 between January 1952 and January 1953. Nearest the camera at the open air Ibrox Garage is DS39 (FYS 344), with DS33, DS35 and DS37 alongside. They were part of GCT's biggest concentration of single-deckers, serving Hillington Industrial Estate to which the main southern access was beneath a low railway bridge. Lowering the road beneath the bridge in May 1964 greatly reduced the need for single-deckers and saw the end of the last 25 DSs in passenger service. Withdrawal began in 1958 and eight were permanent driver trainers by the early 1960s. *Jim Thomson*

The rebodying programme concluded in 1954 with a further 30 double-deckers from East Lancs, built this time at its Blackburn factory. The handsome five-bay coachwork went on Daimler CWA6 chassis new in 1943-46 with utility bodies mainly by Brush, but also Duple, Massey, Northern Counties and Weymann, to create the DR class. All 30 were withdrawn from passenger service in 1962, but some like DR5 (DGG 912) lasted until 1964/65 as driver trainers. Its chassis was new in 1944 with a Weymann body. *Omnibus Society/Roy Marshall*

The Trolleybus Fleet

For different reasons, for much of their existence trolleybuses wore their Glasgow colours in different styles and proportions to motorbuses. When new in 1949/50, the first 64 double-deckers – 30ft long BUT and Daimler six-wheelers with Metro-Cammell bodies to the design of the London Transport Q1 class – were predominantly cream with lower panels in green and just two bands of orange. While green may well have been more practical than orange on the lower panels, cream was a big mistake on roofs that gathered carbon deposits from the trolley booms. Daimler TD22 (FYS 756) is crossing Albert Bridge on route 101 which started in November 1949. Before commercial advertising was carried, the Daimlers displayed the city coat of arms in the cream upper panels. *C Carter*

After experiments with grey, brown and (on one rear roof dome) black, the roofs and rear upper panels of the six-wheelers were repainted green from 1951 onwards, as applied to TB22 (FYS 722) passing a red tram stop in St Vincent Place in the city centre. This is one of the 34 BUTs, the fleetnumber prefix indicating Trolleybus BUT. *Geoffrey Morant*

To tackle the carbon deposit problem, a new trolleybus livery was introduced in 1953, essentially reversing the areas of green and cream on motorbuses, as applied to Daimler CTM6 fleet number TD7 (FYS 741), which also shows the white-on-green destination and service number blinds that also helped identify trolleybuses. The vehicle behind, TD22 or possibly TD26, is in a rare and short-lived variation applied around 1956 with green rather than orange lower panels. The loss of similar TD30 when burnt out in December 1958 meant that although Glasgow bought 195 trolleybuses, the fleet peaked at 194. The last of the Daimlers were withdrawn in 1964. The tram behind is a Glasgow Standard. *Geoffrey Morant*

It was only with the introduction of the spray-painted scheme that double-deck trolleybuses began to wear the same livery as motorbuses, which was applied when vehicles were repainted from 1960 onwards. A gleaming TB5 (FYS 705), a 1949 BUT 9641T, is turning away from Shawfield terminus to head north on route 101, the second trolleybus route. Intermediate destination displays began to be removed in 1958. Fixed window panes have replaced the original half-drop upper-deck front windscreens. In the picture below, TB14 (FYS714) looks careworn as it climbs Royston Road with its destination blind set for the return journey south to Polmadie. A Crossley-bodied BUT is following behind an articulated Austin parcels van of British Road Services. *Tony Belton (upper), Michael Russell (lower)*

For the second phase of its tram-to-trolleybus conversions in 1953, Glasgow bought 20 Sunbeam F4A two-axle double-deckers, its only 27ft trolleys and only examples with electro-pneumatic brakes. These were the first F4As built. As 'S' was already used to identify single-deckers in the fleet numbering system, these were TG1-20, 'G' being for Guy, Sunbeam's parent company. Fifteen Sunbeams, like TG17 (FYS 792) photographed at Riddrie, had Weymann bodies. The Weymann-bodied TGs introduced a simplified livery, without the lower cream band applied to repainted six-wheelers. *Ray DeGroote/ Online Transport Archive*

Caught in the May 1965 evening sunshine, Weymann-bodied TG18 (FYS 793), turns from Cathedral Street into Castle Street working service 102. Behind it and a Central SMT PD2 is Provand's Lordship, built in 1471 and the oldest in the city. The tall building on the right is the Medical Block of the Royal Infirmary. *Paul Creswell*

A rear end view of similar TG15 (FYS 790) repainted in the spray painted livery. The red TB sign in the lower deck rear window was a warning to following trolleybus drivers not to overtake. It is in the Queensfreey Street, Shawfield terminus of route 101, at which alternate journeys turned short of the full southern section to Rutherglen. These 15 Sunbeams were the only Glasgow trolleybuses with a nearside cab door. The metal grille inside the emergency door provided access to maintain trolley heads. The half-tiled entrance to the common stairs of the tenement houses opposite is an example of a 'wally close' always considered a step up in the social scale from those that were merely painted or whitewashed. *Robin Helliar-Symons*

Sunbeams TG1-5 were the only trolleybuses bodied at Alexander's Stirling coachworks. This is TG5 (FYS 780) returning through the city centre to Hampden Garage, a trolleybus-only facility opened in December 1950 and closed when the last trolleybuses ran in May 1967. *Jim Copland*

Only 21 of the trolleybuses, all Leyland-built BUT RETB1s, were single-deck. However, what they lacked in number they more than made up for in novelty. Eleven were Continental-style standee vehicles with seated conductors, which general manager Eric Fitzpayne was keen to try as an alternative to more expensive double-deckers on which many seats were only required at peak periods. TBS7 (FYS 771), photographed on Royston Road in May 1955, was one of 10 new two years earlier with 27-seat rear-entrance, centre-exit East Lancs bodies. They were designed to accommodate 40 standees. Although by 1958 there were trolleybus routes numbered 101 to 108, most of these had substantial overlapping sections and the 103 was the most obscure number of all, used only between 1950 and 1959 for southbound journeys between Riddrie and Hampden Park. *Ray DeGroote*

Below left Taken on 22nd June 1951, this is the prototype, Weymann-bodied TB 35 (FYS 765), later renumbered TBS1, in the Saltmarket near Glasgow Cross. It was exhibited at the Commercial Motor Show at Earls Court, London in September 1950 and in June 1951 had the distinction of being the only trolleybus operated in Edinburgh when it was demonstrated under tram overhead during an international public transport conference – this picture was taken just after its return from Edinburgh. It differed from the other 10 by having a narrower exit door in the front overhang and until June 1952 was numbered TB35. *C Carter*

Below right These trolleybuses ended their days in a unique version of the spray-painted livery, the only single-deckers on which a cream stripe separated the green and yellow. *Tony Belton*

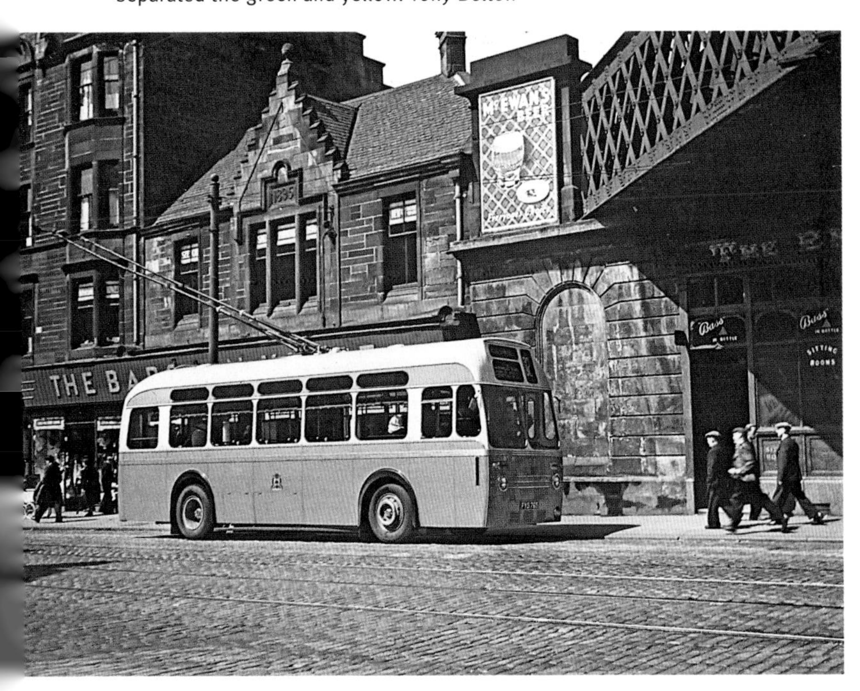

At 34ft 5in, TBS12-21 were Britain's first long single-deckers. When they entered service in November 1958, the maximum permitted length was 30ft and their trial operation paved the way for the introduction of a new 36ft limit in 1961. These 50-seaters, with single-door Burlingham bodies – the only examples of the Blackpool coachbuilder's work in the Glasgow fleet – provided the basic service on the short service 108 linking Paisley Road Toll, where TBS19 (FYS 994) and two others were photographed, with Mount Florida, replacing trams on an inner suburban connection between two of the longer trolleybus routes. Their livery also was unique, with cream window surrounds, green roof and waistband. *Marcus Eavis / Online Transport Archive*

Ninety 30ft two-axle BUT 9613Ts, TB35-124, made up almost half of the trolleybus fleet. They were delivered in 1957/58 for the final phase of the conversion programme and like contemporary motorbuses had three-track number blinds and single-line destination displays. Their chassis were built by Crossley, as were the bodies on the first 71; all 90 bodies were to a Crossley design with frames by Park Royal, which part built 11 and completely built the last eight. Park Royal-bodied TB112 (FYS 873) loads here in Cathcart on a northbound 105 to Queen's Cross, with a similar bus following on service 107 to Maitland Street; the 105 and 107 followed different routes through part of the south side of the city. *Ian Maclean*

TB85 (FYS 846) passing British Railways' Govan Goods Station on the south side of Govan Road from which the Fairfield shipyard's electric locomotive is about to emerge, drawing power from the trolleybus overhead and running on a quarter mile of former tram track to transport steel produced in Lanarkshire into the shipyard. At nearly 10 miles, route 106 from Millerston in the north-east to Bellahouston in the south-west was the longest and busiest trolleybus route, serving densely populated communities, docks, shipyards and other places of industry yet not the city centre. It replaced tram service 7 and was itself replaced by motor bus 65 in October 1966. There is no equivalent 50 years on. *Michael Russell*

Clarkston terminus on 27 May 1967, the final day of trolleybus operation. Crossley-bodied TB65 (FYS 826), still in its original livery and in public service, leads TB78 – now preserved at Sandtoft Trolleybus Museum – in spray-painted livery and specially decorated TB123 (the last trolleybus delivered to Glasgow), both of which were hired by enthusiasts. TB78 was the only trolleybus to wear the reversed livery applied to a few buses in 1964. *Ian Maclean*

Vehicles of the mid-1950s

The 'tin front' era began in Glasgow in 1954 with D67 (FYS 522), an Alexander-bodied Daimler CVG6 exhibited at the Commercial Motor Show in London that September and placed in service two months later as part of an intake of 150 Daimlers, AECs and Leylands. Although there already were 8ft-wide motorbuses and trolleybuses in the fleet, these all were 7ft 6in wide and were the last to come with such luxuries as varnished interior window surrounds. D67 was unique, with a four-bay body similar in outline to those on Sunbeam trolleybuses TG1-5. When new, it had a recessed driver's windscreen, which was replaced well before this photograph was taken in the orange version of the spray-painted livery. It was scrapped in 1969. *Iain MacGregor*

The other 149 of the first 'tin front' double-deckers – 49 of them Daimler CVG6s with Gardner 6LW engines and preselector gearboxes – arrived in 1955/56 with five-bay bodies to a Weymann design. Weymann bodied all 49 Daimlers and supplied D95 (FYS 550) in an experimental unpainted livery with only the bonnet assembly in orange, mudguards black and the wheels and lifeguard in cadmium. It was only two months old when an American tram photographer captured what may well be the only colour image of it in this livery on Royston Road in May 1955. It was repainted in standard green, cream and orange in January 1957. *Ray DeGroote/ Online Transport Archive*

Most numerous of the 150 mid-1950s double-deckers were 75 unusual AEC Regent Vs with preselector gearboxes, Gardner 6LW engines, vacuum brakes and pressed metal grilles. They were among the first Regent Vs built. A338 (FYS 644), new in March 1956, was one of 26 with Weymann bodies. Alexander bodied the other 49 to an identical design, using Weymann frames; the Alexander examples had body numbers for both manufacturers. *Geoffrey Morant*

The remaining 25 were Leyland Titan PD2/25s with Alexander bodies on Weymann frames with dual body numbers. These were the first of 465 postwar Titans, all with air brakes and Pneumo-cyclic two-pedal control transmission, which were allocated fleet numbers directly after those of the 23 rebodied TD4s. This is L37 (FYS 660) operating one of the services connecting employment and shopping at Govan Cross with postwar housing developments in the south-west of the city. *Iain MacGregor*

For its next significant intake of single-deckers, 30 Leyland Royal Tiger Worldmasters were delivered in 1956-58. Like the single-deck Daimlers, they had dual-door bodies completed in GCT workshops, but this time in the tramcar works at Coplawhill. With much of the bus industry then moving to lightweight single-deckers, the Worldmaster was an unusual choice for a British operator. It was a heavy duty export chassis with 150hp Leyland O.680 engine and the semi-automatic Pneumo-cyclic gearbox favoured in the corporation's PD2s. Weymann supplied the body shells, which Coplawhill fitted out as 40-seaters intended to be one-man operated on quieter routes like the 32 between Clarkston and Broomielaw in the city centre, operated from 1957 with Worldmasters like LS6 (FYS 677), new in October 1956. *Jim Thomson*

Agreement was never reached to operate the Worldmasters without conductors, so they were rebuilt as one-door 44-seaters between 1960 and 1963 and painted green and yellow without any relief colour. After the road under Hillington Estate railway bridge was lowered in May 1964, single-deckers were only required for two short suburban routes, the 24 in the north-west and the 30 in the east, the latter being operated by LS1 (FYS 672) before it was cut back from Carmyle to Sandyhills in 1966. Those two routes ran for much of the day with two buses each, and 12 Worldmasters were sold to the Millburn Motors dealership in 1965, LS1 and LS6 in the previous picture being among five operated (as one-man buses) with Southend Corporation from 1966 to 1972. GCT converted LS26 back to two-door layout in 1967 as a spare one-man bus.
Geoffrey Morant

Tram replacement

Besides its normal fleet renewal, GCT replaced its remaining trams with motorbuses between March 1958 and September 1962. To meet this requirement, between November 1956 and the end of 1960 it bought 450 similar looking 61-seat 8ft-wide double-deckers on Leyland and Daimler chassis. The Leylands were Titan PD2/24s with Pneumo-cyclic transmission. Alexander-bodied L165 (SGD 67) entered service in October 1958. Once longer PD3s joined the fleet, the PD2/24s became known to crews as 'wee Ls'.
Jim Thomson

L175 (SGD 77) was one of the first buses painted in a version of the two-colour livery, entering service in October 1958 in green and orange separated only by a black moulding line. It remained in this non-standard style for five years and was photographed when new.
Jim Thomson

L119 (SGD 21) entered service in March 1959 in a lighter green and yellow version of the livery applied to L175 and was joined three months later by five similar buses, all six gaining cream relief bands within three years. These were among 75 PD2/24s bodied at Coplawhill tramcar works using Alexander parts. They could be told apart from the Alexander-built bodies by their thicker window surrounds, similar to those on Liverpool buses. *Jim Thomson*

A specification change in 1958 resulted in 100 of the PD2/24s being supplied with sliding rather than hinged cab doors. These included GCT-bodied L141 (SGD 43) new in November 1959 in the by then standard livery with cream relief. *Jim Thomson*

PD2s under construction at Coplawhill in spring 1959. L127 on the right is one of the six delivered in green and yellow without any cream relief. Beyond the two buses on the left are two partly dismantled Standard trams and towards the back of the workshop is a Subway car from GCT's underground railway. A postwar Cunarder tram is visible to the right of L127. *Jim Thomson*

Alexander-bodied L278 (SGD 280) was among eight PD2/24s repainted towards the end of 1964 in a reversed livery using different shades of yellow and green. This could have proved more practical than having the lighter colour on the lower panels had GCT held its nerve, but such was the public outcry that the experiment was curtailed after just 22 double-deckers (including trolleybus TB78) were repainted and all were restored speedily to standard colours and layout. *Ian Maclean*

All 150 Daimlers had Alexander bodies. D117-216 were CVG6s with preselector gearboxes, hinged cab doors and Birmingham-style 'new look' bonnet assemblies. All were delivered in the green, cream and orange livery and were repainted in the later livery style, as on D207 (SGD 191) operating tram replacement route 57 in 1969. By then this 1958 bus had gained a saloon heater, hence the grille to the nearside of the destination box. *Omnibus Society/ Roy Marshall*

The other 50 of the 150 Daimlers – D218-67 – were new in 1959 with Daimatic semi-automatic gearboxes, Manchester-style glass fibre bonnets and sliding cab doors. Forty-five were CVG6s with Gardner 6LW engines, but the last five were CVD6s with the MkVIII version of Daimler's CD6. The first 25, including D221 (SGD 204) photographed in Jamaica Street at the head of an impressive line of cars and vans in the summer of 1959, were among the last buses delivered in this livery style. *Jim Thomson*

High capacity experiments

Numbered between the two batches of 8ft-wide CVG6s was D217 (FYS 999), GCT's first 30ft long double-decker motor bus and one of two high-capacity buses allocated the highest registration numbers in the FYS series. This was a rare beast, one of two prototype Daimler CVD650-30 chassis with 10.6litre CD650 engine, fully-automatic transmission and power steering. Its five-bay 73-seat Alexander body was a lengthened version of the 61-seat body on the 450 Leylands and Daimlers and it had the wider version of the Manchester-style bonnet. It was exhibited at the Scottish Motor Show in November 1957 and entered service in March 1958. It led an isolated life for its first 11 years, allocated to Langside garage and confined to routes that did not penetrate the city centre. Its main haunt was the inter-suburban 4A (renumbered 34 in March 1961) between Govan Cross and the postwar council housing scheme at Castlemilk, with occasional forays on to peak hour service 29 between Castlemilk and Hillington Estate. This picture shows it at Govan Cross when nearly new, with the Subway station next to the bar on the opposite pavement. It lost its non-standard mechanical features at various overhauls (a Gardner 6LW from an AEC Regent V replaced the CD650 in 1968) and only began venturing into the city centre after the 34 was converted to one-man operation in November 1969. It survived in service until 1975, was acquired for preservation four years later and was briefly in First Glasgow ownership (with national fleet number 39999) in the first decade of the 21st century. Having eluded photographers in its early life, it may now be one of the most photographed preserved Glasgow buses. *Jim Thomson*

If the high-capacity bus registered FYS 999 led an anonymous early life, the one registered FYS 998 was one of the city's most recognised double-deckers – even to people with little interest in buses. This was LA1, one of the pre-production Leyland Atlanteans exhibited at the September 1958 Commercial Motor Show in London and the first Atlantean in Scotland. Its 'wrong way round' positioning of engine and platform were bound to catch folks' attention, especially as this 78-seater was let loose on to busy cross-city routes after initial trials on suburban route 26 between Priesthill and Govan. It holds the distinction of being regarded – officially at least – as the first bus completed at Alexander's then new coachworks in Falkirk. Like Atlanteans built mainly for Tyneside fleets over the next three years, the unequal depth windows and general (lack of) shape of the Alexander body owed more to contemporary Metro-Cammell practice than anything the Scottish coachbuilder produced on front-engined chassis. It also was the only Glasgow double-decker without any nearside route number display, as well as being the sole Atlantean in the green, cream and orange livery and (until its first overhaul) GCT's only one with a single-piece engine cover. *Jim Thomson*

LA1 was upgraded to MkII Atlantean standard with a three-piece engine cover and the centre lower deck windows were replaced by units for newer Atlantean bodies during a later overhaul. It remained in passenger service until it became a driver trainer in March 1973. Its historic significance was recognised and it was retained in preservation, spending around 30 years on display in Glasgow's Museum of Transport. At the time of writing, it is stored in the city museums' resource centre at Nitshill, not far from Priesthill where it first ran in service in December 1958. *Iain MacGregor*

Forward entrance

Given its experience with a fleet of predominantly 30ft-long fleet of trolleybuses, there should have been little surprise that GCT followed the trial purchase of D217 and LA1 by placing a further 229 maximum length double-deckers in service between July 1960 and September 1962. These were 89 AEC Regent Vs and 140 Leyland Titan PD3s, but there was a change of plan between the order and delivery. The original intention was that, like D217, they would have rear entrance bodies. However, a side benefit of scrapping trams was a plan – enacted in November 1963 – to create one-way traffic flows on two east/west and two north/south city centre thoroughfares. That meant buses using all four lanes of these streets and safety concerns led to a 72-seat layout with forward entrances and platform doors. That also altered the specification of the Alexander-bodied Regent Vs, which – like the 75 delivered in 1955/56 – were ordered with Gardner 6LW engines, albeit driving this time through a Monocontrol semi-automatic gearbox. The 6LW is a long engine, which would have intruded on to the front platform, so they came instead with AEC's 9.6-litre AV590. This view in Cathedral Street in the city centre is of A359 (SGD 509), which entered service in March 1961 and was withdrawn in 1972. All but 11 were withdrawn by 1973, victims of a shortage of AEC parts and the poor finish of the bodies, which were weakened by the long rear overhang. *Omnibus Society/Roy Marshall*

The 140 Leylands were largely similar to the AECs, but had air- rather than electrically-operated doors. Coplawhill tramcar works bodied 25 of them over the three-year period it took Alexander's to supply the other 115; slightly different colour shades made the Glasgow-built bodies distinguishable when new but they were otherwise identical. The chassis of 139 of them was the Titan PD3/2 (Pneumo-cyclic gearbox and air brakes, i.e. the same as the PD2s), but one difference from all Titans supplied before or after was their 'Leyland Albion Titan' radiator badges with the blue and white Scottish Saltire – a token salute to the Glasgow manufacturer Leyland had acquired in 1951 and which undertook pre-delivery inspections on Lancashire-built buses after they left the coachbuilder. This is Alexander-bodied L405 (SGD 407), new in November 1960 and one of two surviving in preservation. They suffered from the same body weaknesses as the AECs and many were withdrawn after 12 years, although 49 survived until 1976, a year longer than the last AECs. *Omnibus Society/Roy Marshall*

Odd one out among the Leylands was L398 (SGD 400), exhibited at the 1960 Commercial Motor Show and GCT's sole PD3A/2 with the newly introduced St Helens-style glass fibre bonnet assembly incorporating a cutaway front corner to improve kerbside visibility. The interior of its Alexander body was finished to a higher standard with fluorescent rather than tungsten lighting and cream plastics laminate instead of green-painted metal. Despite that, it was withdrawn in 1972 by which time the distinctive horizontally-slatted radiator grille had been damaged and replaced by a specially cut version with the vertical slats of the other PD3s and PD2s. The 'nearly but not quite' mismatching of many GCT fleet and registration numbers was particularly evident on this bus. *Campbell Sayers*

One further Alexander-bodied 72-seat forward-entrance halfcab double-decker operated with GCT for exactly a year from February 1962 to February 1963. This was 747 EUS, a prototype Albion Lowlander exhibited at the Scottish Motor Show in November 1961 and fitted with a semi-automatic gearbox. Although painted in full GCT livery, it was owned by Albion Motors and went on to spend a further six months on loan to Edinburgh Corporation in a variation of its red and white livery. The Lowlander was a Glasgow-built lowheight version of the Leyland Titan PD3 developed primarily for the Scottish Bus Group. It had a disproportionately high driving position with the four front seats upstairs on raised plinths, an arrangement that looked particularly awkward on the prototypes. GCT had last operated a lowbridge double-decker (a wartime utility Guy Arab) in 1950 and had no obvious need for any more, though its flat floor perhaps had attractions if fitted with a full-height body, while Albion and Leyland may have benefited from subjecting the bus to intensive urban driving. However, GCT had bought its last Albions 10 years earlier and would buy no more halfcab buses. *Iain MacGregor*

The Atlantean era

For its final phase of tram replacement and further bus fleet renewal, GCT had an option to buy a further 153 forward entrance halfcab double-deckers – 78 AEC Regent Vs and 75 Leyland Titan PD3A/2s – but took the bolder and more expensive decision to take 200 Alexander-bodied Leyland Atlanteans, the first of nearly 700 delivered before Greater Glasgow PTE took over. If the 229 forward entrance halfcabs were basic and uninspiring and Atlantean LA1 was box-like in the extreme, these reflected the futuristic aspirations of a decade in which America put a man on the moon and private cars became increasingly desirable consumer products. Thanks to the development of curved, toughened glass and Alexander's investment in glass fibre moulding, the fronts of their A-type bodies incorporated the front and rear windscreens of the Y-type single-decker launched in November 1961, while fluorescent lighting brightened their interiors. Twenty-three were delivered in time to replace the last trams in September 1962 and this photograph shows brand new LA19 (SGD 597) on final replacement service 64 (Dalmuir West-Auchenshuggle) passing Glasgow Cross railway station on the former LMS low level line while tram tracks and overhead wires were still in place. A 1957/58 Daimler CVG6 is on the left, heading north from Saltmarket to High Street on service 37 from Castlemilk to Springburn, the yellow board in the cab (with working timetable on the driver's reverse side) showing it is operating route (duty) 77. Most Atlanteans from LA2 to LA542 had 'Leyland Albion Atlantean' badges. Leyland borrowed LA6 and LA83 to demonstrate to potential Atlantean customers and in March 1963 bought back LA91 and used it for two years as a demonstrator, retaining its Glasgow registration SGD 669. It almost certainly never ran with GCT and nominally was replaced by an additional bus numbered LA202. *Omnibus Society/Roy Marshall*

Having supplied a proportion of Glasgow's fleet requirements until 1959, Daimler was keen to offer the Gardner 6LX-engined Fleetline as an alternative to the Atlantean and in May 1963 delivered D268 (SGD 730) with the registration number between those for LA151 and LA152. It combined a chassis similar to those then being delivered to Midland Red with a flat floor version of the A-type bodies on GCT's Atlanteans and operated alongside Atlanteans at Maryhill garage. Daimler exhibited a second, almost identical bus in full GCT livery at the November 1963 Scottish Motor Show, but the corporation declined to take up the invitation to buy it and that vehicle became demonstrator 565 CRW. Only Leylands would join GCT's fleet for the rest of its existence. Perhaps Daimler should have detected a lack of enthusiasm from the outset from an operator that chose to number its first Atlantean in its own new series in 1958 but tagged this on to the end of an assorted collection of front-engined Daimlers. It saw spasmodic service, grounded for lengthy periods when unique replacement parts needed to be ordered, and in October 1975 – five months after the last CVG6s were withdrawn – GGPTE sold it to Graham's of Paisley, a Fleetline fan that had owned 565 CRW since 1967. The bus that might have become D269 was finally united with D268 and they ran together until 1979. *Iain MacGregor*

Postwar one-man operation finally came in Glasgow in May 1965 when LS31 (CYS 139B), the first of 16 Leyland Panthers with 36ft Alexander W-type bodies, entered experimental service from Newlands garage. After three months on inter-suburban service 40, the trials settled on service 21 between Pollok housing scheme and Midland Street on the southernmost edge of the city centre. This is Pollok terminus, which became an unlikely Mecca for bus enthusiasts in the mid- to late-1960s. All 16 Panthers (and Worldmaster LS26 from 1967) were painted in reversed livery, which helped tell them apart from the crew-operated double-deckers providing most journeys on the 21 until February 1969. LS31 was one of the first Panthers built and had the first W-type body, with two doors, 42 seats and space for 31 standees. It was exhibited at the September 1964 Commercial Motor Show in London and was joined in February 1966 by similar LS32, which had appeared at the November 1965 Scottish Motor Show. LS31 from new and LS32 from May 1966 had two of the first UK bus applications of Voith automatic transmission, the German manufacturer having established a subsidiary in Glasgow in 1962 in the dying days of the North British Locomotive Company. Both of these Panthers had Leyland O.600 engines and an 18ft 6in wheelbase. *Alan Mortimer*

The remaining 14 Panthers, specified by reducing an order for Atlanteans from 150 to 136, had 0.680 engines and 17ft 6in wheelbase. The first of them, LS33 (NUS 834F), was exhibited at the November 1967 Scottish Motor Show and entered service the following February. Like LS31 and LS32, it had a Voith gearbox but its panoramic windows were unique and probably did nothing for the inherently weak structure of a two-door body on a flexible rear-engined chassis. The three Voith-geared Panthers were withdrawn in 1971, which meant that LS33 saw little more than two years' service. This 1970 photograph shows it emerging from the Stygian depths of Midland Street, a dark terminus beneath Glasgow Central railway station where passengers for the south-western housing schemes inhaled a curious mix of fumes of idling bus diesel engines and an aroma of wine or spirits stored in commercial premises. The 'lazy' destination display, with outer and inner termini displayed diagonally on a single line, was typical of early conversions to one-man operation, sparing drivers the need to turn blinds every half hour. Services 21 and 39 were the first to lose all conductors following the end of a lengthy national dispute over bus crews' pay involving employers and trades unions (which would have settled earlier) and the Wilson government's Prices & Incomes Board, which was trying to control inflation. *Omnibus Society/Roy Marshall*

LS35 (PYS 988G) on Glasgow Bridge soon after entering service in February 1969. By the time LS34-46 arrived, Atlanteans were being converted for one-man operation and – as often before – single-deckers were regarded as a non-standard nuisance. These 43-seaters started out on the Pollok routes but most were transferred to Maryhill and Gartcraig garages in spring 1970 to replace crew-operated Worldmasters on services 24 and 30. There was no physical need for single-deckers on the 24, and the 30 was re-routed in 1977 to take double-deckers. Panther numbers declined steadily from 1974, but LS35 was among seven converted to single-door layout in 1975/76 and one of three heavily rebuilt as coaches (with panoramic windows) in 1977 and retained in PTE service until 1981.
Campbell Sayers

GCT began adapting Atlanteans for one-man operation in 1968 and the same year took delivery of LA422, the first of 287 delivered to GCT and GGPTE as dual-door 75-seaters with the front staircase reversed to descend towards the exit door. All were to the increased maximum width of 8ft 2 in (2.5m), but LA422 had an 8ft wide chassis with an engine cover narrower than the main body. It entered service in November 1968 registered PYS 950G but as this picture taken at Alexander's Falkirk factory shows (with a Dundee Corporation AEC Swift just visible on the right), it was completed several months earlier with registration PUS 318F. Centre doors were rarely used on any of these Atlanteans and the door mechanism on this bus was particularly troublesome, requiring a second crew member to pull them open when it entered service on the 21. Centre doors were removed from Atlanteans in PTE ownership from 1974 onwards.
Alan Mortimer

Atlantean LA143 (SGD 721) adapted for one-man operation and working inter-suburban service 8, which lost conductors in May 1969. It displays two features of those early one-man conversion: an orange dot on the front dome and a barely legible "lazy" destination display showing both terminals. *Omnibus Society/Harry Hay*

Dual-door LA472 (UGA 225H) of a batch licensed in September 1969. In this case the orange dot has been peeled off to reveal a brighter circle of green. *Omnibus Society/Roy Marshall*

In March 1972, Atlantean LA230 (CYS 576B) became the first bus in Scotland to appear in an overall advertising livery as part of a national campaign by Barclaycard. It publicised the credit cards for nearly two years, changing halfway through this period into an orange-based livery. *Iain MacGregor*

Atlanteans from LA601 upwards, introduced from late 1972, were to the improved AN68 specification with Alexander's square-profiled alloy-framed AL-type body. This is LA624 (FUS 144L) crossing Glasgow Bridge. The projection above the route number box is the base of the aerial for its two-way radio, a feature introduced primarily for crew security. *Omnibus Society/Roy Marshall*

Into the PTE

Greater Glasgow PTE was keen to give the Glasgow bus fleet a completely new identity, but the Glasgow-dominated passenger transport authority insisted on retaining green and yellow. The result was a compromise, combining the white roofs and window surrounds imported from Edinburgh by director general Ronald Cox with new British Standard shades of Sunglow yellow and Verona green, the latter later adopted by the PTEs in Merseyside and West Yorkshire. This was Alexander-bodied Leyland Titan PD3/2 L481 (SGD 483), which spent two months in the spring of 1974 as a mobile exhibition unit publicising the May elections for the new two-tier local authorities for Glasgow District and Strathclyde Region, before returning to passenger service. After 80 years' existence, the new councils consigned Glasgow Corporation to history in May 1975.
Alan Millar

Only two of the 100 1957/58 Daimler CVG6s with preselector gearboxes were painted in Greater Glasgow PTE livery before the last were withdrawn in 1975. They operated mainly from Larkfield, Langside and Newlands garages in the city's South Side but D169 (SGD 153), the first of the pair to don the new colours, had migrated latterly to Parkhead in the East End and was operating the long cross-city tram replacement 61 route through heavily redeveloped Cowcaddens in the north of the city centre in this picture taken in 1974.
Alan Millar

Edinburgh

If one word describes Edinburgh's municipal buses it is 'stately'. The sober livery of near equal proportions of madder (dark red) and white lined out in gold gave that quality to practically any vehicle it adorned, even 300 otherwise utilitarian Metro-Cammell Orion-bodied Leylands supplied in the mid-1950s.

Those colours seemed at one with Scotland's capital city, as much part of the urban environment as the Georgian architecture of its 18th century New Town and the 16th century Old Town stretching along the Royal Mile between the imposing castle and Holyrood Palace.

They also fit with Edinburgh being the first Scottish municipality to introduce motorbuses – six single-deckers operated on a Southern Circular route started on 3 August 1914 and operated on its behalf by the Edinburgh & District Tramways Company, which ran the city's cable-hauled trams until its lease expired in June 1919.

The timing of this venture was unfortunate in the extreme, for Britain declared war on Germany the day after the Southern Circular started and the route was withdrawn on 1 November, by which time three of the buses had already been commandeered by the military.

It took until 1919 – still ahead of the other cities – for motorbus operations to resume (directly by Edinburgh Corporation Tramways, later Edinburgh Corporation Transport) with an initial fleet of 15 Leyland single-deckers. Three were charabancs for city tours, the other dozen 31-seat single-deck buses for routes complementing the soon-to-be-electrified tram service.

Buses played a temporary tram replacement role during the electrification programme, which also saw the neighbouring Burgh of Leith absorbed into Edinburgh in November 1920 along with its electric municipal trams. But just as in Glasgow, buses played second fiddle to a tram system that continued to be expanded until the outbreak of war in 1939.

Although the fleet expanded throughout the 1920s, it was largely single-deck with a handful of open-top double-deckers. Feeder buses connected with tram routes and pioneered potential tramway extensions, but buses grew gradually in importance as services were introduced to serve new council housing schemes built around the city in the 1920s and 1930s. The first covered-top double-decker arrived in 1933, but it was not until November 1935 that larger scale operation of highbridge double-deckers began.

There were 215 buses in 1939 and trams continued to dominate the ECT fleet, for which 600 buses were purchased between 1919 and 1951. The tide turned swiftly with the decision to replace the trams between June 1952 and November 1956 with over 400 new and second-hand buses, most of them double-deckers.

ECT's bus purchasing choices passed through distinct phases: mainly Leylands and AECs in the 1920s, Daimlers in the 1930s, Daimlers and Guys in the 1940s and predominantly Leylands from 1952 onwards, as well as Bedford coaches for city tours and private hires.

Although it experimented with simplified liveries in the 1950s, ECT kept its buses in traditional madder and white to the end of its existence, but adopted the city's colours of black and white for coaches from 1955.

Save for a new coat of arms and change in legal lettering, the colours were unaltered after operations transferred to Lothian Region Transport in May 1975. Since 2010, council-owned Lothian Buses has adopted a dark red (called 'wein rot' rather than madder), white and gold livery, heavily influenced by the traditional colours.

Princes Street, the principal city centre thoroughfare, in 1975. The leading corporation bus heading east on route 44 is dual-door Alexander-bodied Leyland Atlantean PDR1A/1 320 new in 1969. Next is one of 300 Leyland Titan PD2/20s with Metro-Cammell Orion body, then one of 50 PD2A/30s with Alexander body with a Duple Dominant-bodied Bedford coach directly behind. Today, this street is car-free and tram tracks have been restored to the centre lanes. *Omnibus Society/Roy Marshall*

Edinburgh squeezed long lives out of its prewar Daimler single-deckers, some of which survived as late as 1959 on the high-frequency 21 circular service that ran under low railway bridges. A case in point is 643 (WS 9521), one of 11 Weymann-bodied COG5s new in 1936 and rebuilt by ECT in 1948-50. WS was the registration mark for the Burgh of Leith from 1903 until 1920 when it lost its independence to Edinburgh, which issued WS registrations from 1934 until the 1974 reorganisation transferred WS to Bristol. *Ian Dunnett/Online Transport Archive*

Like many Scottish operators, Edinburgh specified its half cab single-deckers with rear entrances and open platforms. Typical of these was 691 (FSC 157), a Daimler CVG5 with 35-seat Metro-Cammell body new in 1949 and retained until 1961. The location is Tollcross, south-west of the city centre, in May 1955 and the A. Massey & Sons shop was part of a large grocery and greengrocery chain that thrived across central Scotland before the rise of supermarkets. *Ray DeGroote/Online Transport Archive*

The last new half cab single-deckers were 15 Bristol L6Bs with 35-seat Brockhouse bodies built in Clydebank. They arrived in 1950 and lasted 10 years. This is 872 (FWS 165). The chassis, with manual gearbox and Bristol's own AVW engine, were among the last supplied to a municipal customer after the terms of state ownership restricted Bristol to meeting a proportion of the British Transport Commission's requirement for new vehicles. They were a surprising choice for ECT, which hitherto had only two wartime Bristols (with Gardner engines) allocated by the Ministry of Supply. *Ian Dunnett/ Online Transport Archive*

Thirty-three Guy Arab double-deckers were delivered between 1943 and 1946, 22 of them bodied by Northern Counties and 30 on the Arab II chassis. In recognition of the city's hilly terrain, all had Gardner 6LW engines. This is 97 (ESC 924), which entered service in September 1946 and was among the last withdrawn in 1961. A later Northern Counties-bodied Arab III is in the background, both buses carrying advertisements promoting mass X-ray campaigns in the public health fight against tuberculosis. *Ian Dunnett/Online Transport Archive*

There were 15 Northern Counties-bodied Arab IIIs, also with 6LW engines, new in 1949 and 1951 and kept until 1962. This is 200 (GSG 445) one of five new in 1949. Commercial advertising was carried on bus sides from the early 1950s, handled by the Cowan-Ad agency whose name and flag logo is applied between the Capstan advertisement and the route number box above the platform. *Ian Dunnett/Online Transport Archive*

Besides the Guys, ECT took delivery of 17 wartime Daimlers and in 1947 followed them with seven Daimler CVD6s with Northern Counties bodies to a relaxed utility design. This view on Johnston Terrace on the south side of Edinburgh Castle Rock shows 110 (FSC 987), which was withdrawn in 1960. *Ian Dunnett/ Online Transport Archive*

The most numerous type of double-deckers bought in the immediate postwar period were 72 Daimlers (10 CVD6 and 62 CVG6) with Metro-Cammell bodies to Birmingham City Transport design. They were delivered in 1949/50. This is CVG6 163 (GSF 994) turning into Princes Street in front of a Beardmore taxi. *Phil Tatt/Online Transport Archive*

The Birmingham-style Daimlers had the West Midlands city's straight staircase with offside platform window. CVG6 161 (GSF 992), placed in service in January 1950 and withdrawn in 1964, is passing the R. W. Forsyth outfitters in Princes Street. The last five of these Daimlers were withdrawn in 1967. *Phil Tatt/Online Transport Archive*

As non-standard as the 15 Brockhouse-bodied Bristol single-deckers were 17 AEC Regent IIIs from the same bodybuilder, to Park Royal design, in 1950/51. Although it bought 57 AECs between 1920 and 1929, ECT only took three of its products in the intervening years. These Regents, with preselector gearboxes, were all sold for scrap in 1960. This is 231 (HSG 181). *Ian Dunnett/Online Transport Archive*

ECT operated city tours from the start of continuous operations in 1919 and adopted black and white as its coach livery in 1955. X23 (GWS 467) was one of seven Duple Vista-bodied Bedford OB 29-seaters new in 1949/50. The four rings logo on the radiator grille highlights that all seven had their original Bedford petrol engines replaced by Perkins P6 diesels in 1952. They were withdrawn in 1959. ECT was allocated 20 Bedford OWB utility buses in 1942/43 and eight of these were rebodied as similar Vista coaches in 1949, fitted with Perkins diesel engines in 1952 and kept until 1958. Coaches were the last vehicles allocated fleetnumber prefixes in a system introduced in 1935 and phased out on buses in 1951. Besides X for coaches, single-deck buses had an A prefix and double-deckers a G. *Ian Dunnett/ Online Transport Archive*

Tram replacement

Replacement of Edinburgh's trams began in 1952 with an initial stated intention of closing only a quarter of the network but that escalated rapidly to replacement of the entire system. With new general manager Moris Little appointed in 1948, not only were trams scrapped but a fundamental change of purchasing policy saw ECT standardise as much as possible on Leylands. It had bought 98 Leylands between 1919 and 1929 but they and a solitary 'unfrozen' Titan TD7 allocated in 1942 had all departed when the new era began. The new Leylands included the last open rear platform rear-entrance single-deckers built for any of the Scottish cities, Royal Tiger PSU1/13s with Leyland's own 40-seat bodywork. They were used initially on the first tram-to-bus conversion to Comely Bank, north-west of the city centre, in June 1952 but within five weeks were displaced by double-deckers. This 1958 view shows 812 (HWS 777) at the Granton terminus of route 17 shortly before it was converted into a front-entrance 43-seat one-man bus. The building on the right is HMS Claverhouse, the former Granton Hotel requisitioned in September 1939 for military training. *Geoffrey Morant*

The all-Leyland Royal Tigers were all rebuilt as 37- or 41-seat forward-entrance coaches between 1958 and 1960, with a centre offside emergency door fitted when the open rear platforms were removed. This picture on Waverley Bridge shows 818 (HWS 783). All were withdrawn in 1966 after which this one saw further service with a building contractor in East Lothian. *Geoffrey Morant*

Also new in 1952 were 21 Leyland-bodied Titan PD2/12 56 or 58 seaters acquired from dealer stock and fitted with ECT destination displays before entering service between January and December that year. A Mk2 Ford Zephyr is overtaking 253 (KFS 944) at the West End as they turn out of Princes Street into Queensferry Street. *Ian Dunnett/Online Transport Archive*

All 21 of these PD2/12s were heavily refurbished in 1961/62 as 59-seaters with additional seats downstairs and fitted with glass fibre versions of Leyland's full-width bonnet. The transformation left them looking more like the 100 Midland Red LD8 class Titan PD2/20s of 1952/53, the first Leyland double-deckers with this style of concealed radiator. One of the first to emerge from rebuilding was 242 (JSF 657), photographed in Princes Street around the time of the state visit of King Olaf V of Norway in October 1962. They were withdrawn in 1970, after that year's Commonwealth Games were held in the city, which had created a temporary requirement for additional buses. *Alan Mortimer*

Arguably the most remarkable of all of Edinburgh's tram replacement buses were 60 wartime utility Guy Arabs acquired from London Transport in 1952/53, reconditioned, rebodied and re-registered as new vehicles. Reconstruction widened them to 8ft. Their 55-seat lightweight full-front bodies (without nearside glazing to the engine area) were built by Duple, with most completed by its Nudd Brothers & Lockyer subsidiary at Kegworth that later became Duple Midland. All retained their Gardner 5LW engines, which limited their performance on the city's hills, though one was fitted with a 6LW engine in 1963. This May 1955 view in Princes Street (with the Sir Walter Scott monument behind) shows 312 (JWS 592) operating route 33, which replaced tram service 3 in March 1953. It is in original condition with ornate radiator grille and was based on the chassis of London Transport G314. Tram 156 alongside it was built at ECT's Shrubhill works in 1931. *Ray DeGroote/Online Transport Archive*

The ex-London Guys were fitted with ECT's favoured glass fibre Leyland-style fronts in 1957/58, as exemplified by 352 (JWS 632). This was based on London Transport G173. *Geoffrey Morant*

An offside view of ex-London Transport Guy 359 (JWS 639) in St Andrew Square. This was based on London Transport G155. Most were withdrawn in 1967, but 359 was among 20 kept in service until early 1969. *Alan Mortimer*

In 1954, ECT followed the reconstruction of the ex-London Guys with a similar modernisation of the 16 surviving examples of its wartime utility Daimlers new in 1943-45. Two of these had CWG5 chassis with Gardner 5LW engines while the others all were CWA6s with 7.7litre AEC engines. It repowered the 14 CWA6s with 5LW engines and had 8ft-wide 58-seat full-front (again no nearside glazing to the engine area) Alexander bodies fitted. Like the Brockhouse-bodied Bristol L6B single-deckers, they had sliding cab doors, though ECT standardised on hinged doors on front-engined double-deckers up to and including the final examples in 1966. They began life with flat chrome-embellished grilles but in 1959 were fitted with Leyland-style glass fibre fronts similar to those on the Guys, as on 78 (EFS 133) new in February 1945 with a Brush body, photographed on North Bridge. It was sold for scrap in 1967 along with the last of these unusual double-deckers. *Ian Dunnett/ Online Transport Archive*

The Orions

The biggest part of the tram replacement fleet comprised 300 Leyland Titan PD2/20s (manual gearboxes, vacuum brakes) with lightweight Metro-Cammell Orion bodies placed in service between May 1954 and November 1957. This September 1958 photograph taken in The Mound in the city centre shows 592 (LWS 592), new in October 1955. The Spartan specification of these buses drew unfavourable comparison with the trams that most of them replaced, one member of the corporation famously commenting at the time that 'they are ungainly, inelegant, monstrous masses of shivering tin – they are modern to the extent of being able to produce a perfect synchronisation of rock n' roll'. Despite the criticism, they proved highly durable and 516 gave 20 years' service. The Orions were the first buses with matching fleet and registration numbers. *Geoffrey Morant*

This June 1955 photograph taken at Granton shows 63-seat Orion 516 (LWS 516), which entered service two months earlier when bus route 8 replaced the tram route of the same number. It is in original condition with two-line intermediate destination display and limited upper saloon ventilation. Shrubhill-built tram 173 behind was new in 1936. *Geoffrey Morant*

Driver training buses began to be distinguished from regular service buses in 1973 when this brighter livery with more white and less madder was applied to some Orion-bodied PD2/20s. Among them was T3 (NSF 731), the former 731 new in August 1956, photographed later in 1973 passing a selection of British-built cars of the period. *Omnibus Society/Roy Marshall*

Eleven of the Orion-bodied PD2/20s ran in unpainted 'silver' until repainted in standard madder and white in 1959. They were panelled in Birmabright, a sheet metal alloy of aluminium and magnesium also used in Land Rovers and produced by Birmingham-based Birmetals. The first of the 11 appeared in 1955 and was completely unpainted, followed by 10 of the 39 Orions placed in service after the trams were withdrawn. They had a madder waistband and among them was 798 (OFS 798), first used in November 1957 and withdrawn 20 years later. It has the increased upper deck ventilation retrofitted on earlier examples. This picture shows it at Portobello Town Hall. 798 is now in preservation at the Scottish Vintage Bus Museum, finished in madder and white. *Ian Dunnett/Online Transport Archive*

ECT increased the size of intermediate destination boxes in the 1960s to accommodate up to six places in upper and lower case lettering. The effect is apparent on Orion-bodied PD2/20 757 (NSF 757) photographed leaving Queensferry Street onto Dean Bridge in May 1974; around a year later this 1956 example was sold to a training company. *Geoffrey Morant*

The other deliveries of the 1950s

ECT returned to Guy for one last time with 70 Alexander-bodied Arab IVs new between November 1955 and December 1956 as part of the tram replacement programme. These 63-seaters, like 923, climbing North St Andrew Street, passing The Traveller's Tryst pub owned by the Scottish Bus Group and next to the bus station entrance, bore a close resemblance to 100 Alexander-bodied Daimler CVG6s delivered soon after to Glasgow, but their tuneful constant mesh gearboxes made them appear obsolescent from the start and helped hasten their withdrawal ahead of the synchromesh-geared PD2/20s, as their departure shortened the amount of time needed to train new recruits. Most were withdrawn in 1972, but some came off as early as 1969. Besides being Edinburgh's last Guys, they also were its last non-Leyland double-deckers. *Geoffrey Morant*

With tram replacement completed, ECT bought only six new double-deckers between the arrival of the last Orion-bodied PD2s in 1957 and the resumption of larger scale double-deck renewal in 1961/62. Those six 72-seat Alexander-bodied Leyland Titans were its first 30ft long and first forward-entrance vehicles. The first of the six, 998 (PWS 998), was the most unusual. This PD3/2 with Pneumo-cyclic automatic transmission and air brakes had a unique glass fibre bonnet and grille developed jointly by Alexander's and truck cab manufacturer Holmes of Preston to offer drivers better kerbside visibility than was possible with the standard bonnet developed for Midland Red. It was the last ECT bus supplied with a sliding cab door. In this view in Pilton, the substantial grab handle for drivers is clearly visible within the false window on the staircase panel. *Ian Dunnett/Online Transport Archive*

The other PD3/2 in the sextet was 999 (PWS 999), like 998 a 1957 chassis but this was not delivered until March 1959. The original plan was for Metro-Cammell to body it with the forward-entrance derivative of the Orion. It spent its first three years in this experimental red livery relieved only by two gold lines above and below the lower saloon windows. The rear end of the body of this and the other four PD3s built at the same time was much less rounded than that on 998 and the lower saloon emergency exit was relocated from the rear overhang to directly behind the staircase. *Ian Dunnett/Online Transport Archive*

The sextet was completed in 1959 by four PD3/3 Titans with synchromesh gearboxes and vacuum brakes. One of these, 264 (SWS 264), carried another livery variation with more madder and less white until 1962. Guy Arab IV 959 had a cherry red version of this style from 1959 to early 1961. *Ian Dunnett/Online Transport Archive*

PD3/3 261 (SWS 261) entering a seemingly empty St Andrew Square in 1964. In 1971, 261-4 were renumbered 994-7 to make way for new Leyland Atlanteans. In March 1974, ECT sold all six of these PD3s to the Scottish Bus Group's Highland Omnibuses, which used them for the next two-and-a-half years on town services in Inverness. *Omnibus Society/Roy Marshall*

A new single-deck fleet

ECT's priority at the end of the 1950s was to replace its assorted fleet of non-standard and in some cases prewar half cab single-deckers. In 1959/60, it bought 100 Weymann-bodied Leyland Tiger Cub PSUC1/3s with Pneumo-cyclic transmission. This 1968 photograph shows 87 (VSC 87) from the second batch of 50 delivered in 1960, most of which had 47 seats incorporating a 3+2 layout towards the back. The first 50 led short lives in Edinburgh, two written off with accident damage in 1963 and the other 48 made redundant in 1966 following removal of the low bridge clearances that had restricted the high-frequency 1 (formerly 21) Clermiston Circle to single-deckers; those 48 were sold to the Ulster Transport Authority to help modernise the fledgling Ulsterbus fleet. Fifteen of the 1960 buses were withdrawn by the end of ECT's existence in 1975, but no.87 survived until 1978. *Geoffrey Morant*

Leyland Leopard PSU3/2R 101 (YSG 101), with the first of over 3,260 Y-type bodies built by Alexander, was exhibited at the November 1961 Scottish Motor Show and entered service in April 1962. General manager Moris Little took advantage of the newly permitted 36ft (11m) length limit to take up where Glasgow had left off with its standee trolleybuses in the 1950s and bring continental European practice to Edinburgh. It had 33 seats, a seated conductor and a three-door layout, with a double-width rear entrance, single-width centre and front exits. Like the Glasgow trolleybuses, it might have stood a chance of working had there been sufficient similar buses to convert an entire route, but as a one-off among double-deckers on route 16 it confused and failed to catch on. *J T Inglis*

In 1969 it was converted into a 45-seat single-door vehicle for the then one-bus shuttle service between Edinburgh Airport and the city centre and painted in black and white coach livery. It became a one-man-operated bus in madder and white in 1975 and survived in Lothian Region Transport ownership until April 1988 when it was sold for preservation and restored to its original three-door layout. *Geoffrey Morant*

The coach fleet was upgraded with 22 new Duple-bodied Bedfords in 1963/64. Four of them, including 203 (203 SC) at the city tour departure point on Waverley Bridge, were VAS1s with 25-seat Bella Vista bodies. This led a surprisingly long life in the fleet, delivered in May 1963 and sold in March 1982. *Omnibus Society/Roy Marshall*

Twelve Duple Bella Vega-bodied Bedford SB5s included 219 (219 SC) and 209 (209 SC) new in May 1963. They are at the north end of Waverley Bridge, with Princes Street Gardens on the right. There also were six twin-steer Bedford VALs with Duple Vega Major bodies. *Omnibus Society/ Roy Marshall*

1960s double-deckers

The first volume intake of new double-deckers in four years saw 50 Alexander-bodied Leyland Titan PD2A/30 66-seaters delivered between December 1961 and March 1962. They were ECT's last open rear platform buses and its last 27ft double-deckers. The chassis, with vacuum brakes and synchromesh gearboxes, were supplied to Shrubhill works with framing for Leyland's then standard St Helens-style glass fibre bonnet and grille, with cutaway for kerbside visibility. Shrubhill fitted its own glass fibre version of Leyland's Midland Red-specified bonnet assembly before dispatching them to Falkirk for bodying. This September 1968 photograph outside St Andrew Square bus station shows 632 (YWS 632), equipped from new with an illuminated advertisement panel, passing a Commer PB newspaper delivery van for *The Scotsman* and *Evening News*. The march of one-person operation meant these buses led shorter lives than the older Orion PD2s, 632 being withdrawn in 1976. Twelve others were sold the following year to Eastern Scottish, which was experiencing an acute shortage of serviceable vehicles. *Geoffrey Morant*

The next 50 double-deckers, new between June and October 1964, were 70-seat Alexander-bodied Leyland Titan PD3/6s, ECT's last with vacuum brakes and synchromesh gearboxes. These chassis were delivered to Shrubhill with exposed radiators and were fitted with glass fibre Midland Red-style bonnets and grilles before bodying. In September 1968, the third of the batch, 653 (ASC 653B), was pictured heading west along Princes Street. *Omnibus Society/Roy Marshall*

After its year in Glasgow, prototype Alexander-bodied Albion Lowlander 747 EUS operated with ECT between March and October 1963 on the 19 Circle, painted in a lighter red version of fleet livery that also disguised the high driving position by the application of white relief only to the roof and upper deck window surrounds. It was the only bus in the ECT fleet to run in service with Leyland's St Helens-style glass fibre bonnet and grille. At the time, lowheight double-deckers were seen as a possible solution for busy routes negotiating low bridges in the city, and a year earlier ECT had bought another prototype Lowlander chassis, which was stored unbodied, then sold back to Albion in June 1964 and on to Western SMT. Here 747 EUS ascends North St Andrew Street while a Scottish Omnibuses Bristol Lodekka progresses eastwards from Queen Street into York Place. *Omnibus Society/Roy Marshall*

Edinburgh initially resisted the tidal wave of overall advertisement opportunities and had PD3/6 673 (ASC 673B) decorated with the compromise of what was known as a broadside advert, applied only to the upper panels to promote Cutty Sark whisky. The effect was a little like an Edinburgh version of Greater Glasgow PTE colours. *Omnibus Society/Roy Marshall*

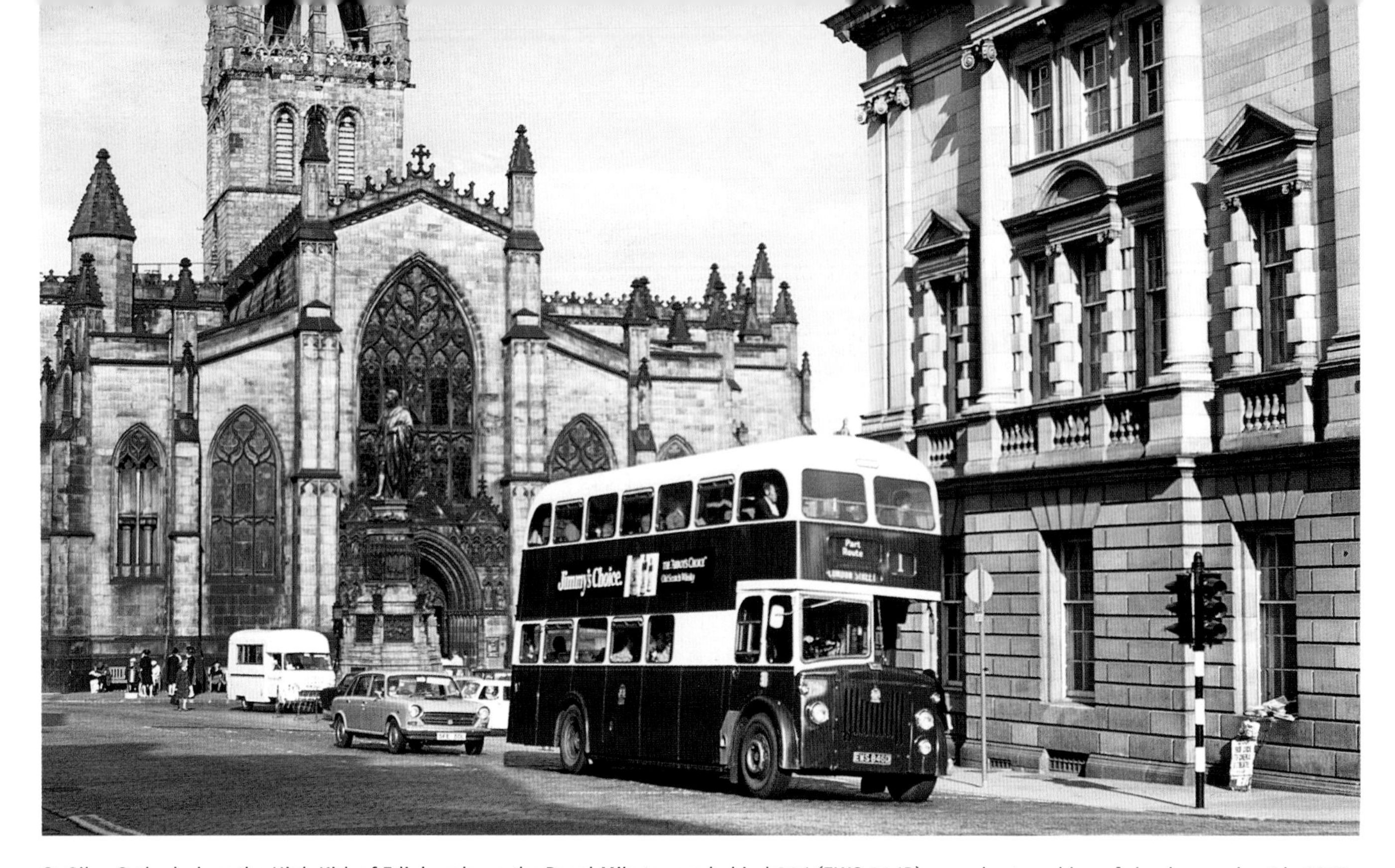

St Giles Cathedral, or the High Kirk of Edinburgh, on the Royal Mile towers behind 846 (EWS 846D) on a short working of circular service 1 in 1973. There were 25 of these Titan PD3A/2s with Pneumo-cyclic transmission and air brakes (Shrubhill bonnet assemblies fitted in place of frames for St Helens-style Leyland units) delivered between June and September 1966 to replace Tiger Cubs on the 1. These last half cab double-deckers for any of the Scottish municipals were not meant to have been. Ronald Cox, who moved from Bournemouth to become ECT general manager in 1964, wanted rear-engined buses and intended to split orders 50/50 between the Leyland Atlantean and Daimler Fleetline. He got his first 25 Atlanteans, but canny councillors opted for these PD3s in place of the Fleetlines. They were withdrawn in 1978/79, though some of the 1964 PD3s remained in service until conductor operation ended in October 1980. *Omnibus Society/Roy Marshall*

Ronald Cox may not have got all the rear-engined double-deckers he wanted in 1966, but he ensured that Edinburgh's Alexander-bodied Leyland Atlanteans bore a stamp of his ideas about vehicle design. These included twin-leaf rather than four-leaf doors, and disguising the cutaway bustle effect of the engine by specifying side fairings. Twenty-three of them had short windows with sliding vents – one was 803 (EWS 803D) photographed turning from South St Andrew Street onto Princes Street in October 1969. *Omnibus Society/Roy Marshall*

The other Ronald Cox design feature, executed on the first two of the 1966 buses and on all delivered from 1967 onwards, was to create panoramic windows with alternate pillars omitted to let in more light. This is 873 (JSC 873E) from the 1967 delivery with an Eastern Scottish Bristol Lodekka behind it pulling out of St Andrew Square bus station. *Geoffrey Morant*

The 50th Atlantean in the 1967 delivery, 900 (JSC 900E), was the first 33ft PDR2/1 version built and could easily be distinguished by the extra, short side windows at the back of the top deck and by the fact that the offside main window pillars were in the same place on both decks, unlike on the shorter PDR1s and later AN68s. It had 82 seats, against 74 on the other single-door Atlanteans. Although exhibited at the November 1967 Scottish Motor Show, it did not enter service until April 1968 by which time its E-suffix registration was several months out of date. The Edinburgh motor taxation office seemed relaxed about such matters, as half of the JSC-E batch entered service after the suffix letter changed to F on 1 August 1967 and both ECT and Eastern Scottish were permitted to use 'stale' pre-booked registrations in subsequent years. This picture was taken in 1973, two years after 900 was converted for one-person operation. The black-on-white dots either side of the destination display read 'PAY ON ENTRY'. It was converted into an open-top city tours bus and is preserved in that condition. *Omnibus Society/ Roy Marshall*

All new Atlanteans from 1969 onwards had 75-seat dual-door bodies with the exit door directly behind the front axle. In all, 150 PDR1 and PDR1A models with Alexander J-type bodies, like 368 (SSF 368H) new in June 1970 in time for the Commonwealth Games, arrived between 1969 and 1971. When photographed in Princes Street in 1975, the black dot signs either side of the destination box had been changed to coin-in-slot blue arrows for the Autofare exact fare system introduced to reduce the time buses spent at stops. *Omnibus Society/Roy Marshall*

Atlanteans delivered from late 1972 onwards were of the improved AN68 design with the more square profile Alexander AL-type body, of which 150 were delivered before ECT transformed into Lothian Region Transport in May 1975. This 1973 photograph of then new 10 (BFS 10L) on Princes Street shows the mismatched offside pillar arrangement on most Edinburgh Atlanteans. *Geoffrey Morant*

More coaches and single deckers

Edinburgh bought 10 Seddon Pennine IV-236 25-seat midibuses in 1973, using the first of them to launch the short Dumbiedykes Circle service connecting new housing at the foot of Holyrood Road with St Andrew Square in the city centre. The first four of these manual gearbox buses had single rear wheels but they were converted to the twin wheel layout of the other six to improve road holding. This picture taken soon after it entered service in May 1973 is of 107 (CFS 107L) from the second batch. All wore a modified livery with madder confined to the grille and body skirt. The combination of four-cylinder Perkins engines, ticket machines with change trays and granite setts on part of the route made a ride in these little buses incredibly noisy. ECT struggled to find suitable work for all of them and when new five were lent to SELNEC PTE. All were withdrawn in 1980. *Omnibus Society/Roy Marshall*

ECT followed its purchase of six twin-steer Bedford VAL coaches in 1963 with a further nine, all with Duple Viceroy bodies, between 1968 and 1970. Photographed in October 1969 at a municipal bus manager's conference at Gleneagles Hotel, this is fleet number 224 (MSF 224F), a VAL70 new in June 1968 and sold in April 1975. There also were two Ford R226s and four Bedford VAMs also with Viceroy bodies. *Omnibus Society/ Roy Marshall*

Bedford began replacing its front-engined coach chassis in 1970 with its Y-series models with vertical mid engines and ECT followed its purchase of five 45-seat YRQs in 1971 with five 51-seat YRTs in July 1972, all with Duple Viceroy bodies. YRT 243 (AFS 243K) catches late afternoon sun on Waverley Bridge when new, with an AN68 Atlantean behind. It was withdrawn in 1979. *Omnibus Society/Roy Marshall*

Five Duple Dominant-bodied Bedford YRTs followed in 1973. As they qualified for New Bus Grant, paying 50% of the purchase price, they had to operate a proportion of mileage on stage carriage routes, which 215 (NSG 215M) is doing here at Torphin terminus on route 9. *Gavin Booth*

ECT's last 10 new single-deckers, delivered in the first months of 1975, were Bedford YRTs with 49-seat dual purpose Alexander Y-type bodies for city tours, clocking up their bus grant mileage on routes such as the 9, mainly on Sundays. They entered service in coach livery but were later repainted white and madder for use exclusively as buses. Some were subsequently reseated as buses and all were sold in 1981/82. This is 115 (GSX 115N). *Gavin Booth*

Aberdeen

In the 1960s, Aberdeen Corporation Transport was held up as a model of municipal efficiency. While its counterparts farther south lost money or struggled to break even, it delivered a perfect combination of low fares and modest profits.

In this it helped that, since 1958, all operations were centred on a single depot at King Street, around two thirds of a mile north of the city centre, and that its fleet of around 250 buses was more standardised than those in Glasgow, Edinburgh or Dundee.

And we are talking of pre-oil Aberdeen, a city that owed more to the fish that came out of the North Sea than the black gold that would transform its economy from the 1970s onwards, swell and enrich its population and spread it out into new suburbs. That change also accelerated the rise of the private car, creating levels of traffic congestion that did not trouble the bus service before, and made it harder than ever to recruit skilled labour.

Aberdeen was second to Edinburgh in introducing motorbuses, four Thornycroft single-deckers coming in 1920. The first of these operated a city tour from 19 July that year and the first public bus service, between Castle Street and the city centre and Footdee (pronounced 'Fittie'), began on 10 January 1921.

By 1930, the fleet had grown to around 70 buses. Double-deck operation started that year and tram-to-bus route conversions began in 1931, although sections of the tram system were extended until 1938. There were around 100 buses by the outbreak of war in 1939. The last new trams arrived in 1949, but line closures followed from 1951, ending in May 1958 with the busy north/south Bridge of Don-Bridge of Dee route.

As in Edinburgh, there were distinct phases when particular manufacturers were favoured: Thornycroft, Albion and Crossley at various points until 1935, AEC and Daimler from 1936 until 1972, Leyland in increasing quantities from 1966 onwards.

The livery remained green and cream throughout ACT's existence, though there were changes in shades and proportions, and until the final version was adopted in 1964 roofs were painted grey.

Local government reform saw operations transfer to the new Grampian Regional Transport in May 1975, with a revised livery. As an arm's length company, it was sold to its management and employees in January 1989 to become the nucleus of GRT Bus Group, which merged in 1995 with Badgerline to become FirstBus, later FirstGroup. The former ACT operation became First Aberdeen and at the time of writing, King Street depot housed First's global headquarters.

Guild Street in the city centre runs a few hundred yards to the south of Union Street, traditionally Aberdeen's main shopping street, and passes the railway station and out-of-town bus station. This March 1974 photograph shows Alexander-bodied Daimler Fleetline 106 (ERG 106D) of 1966 heading westwards while an AEC Swift with Alexander W-type body is pointing east. Many of Aberdeen's buildings are made of locally-quarried granite, hence it being known as the 'Silver City'. *Omnibus Society/ Roy Marshall*

Twenty wartime utility Daimlers – 14 CWA6, two CWG5 and four CWD6 – were allocated between 1943 and 1945, and thanks to major body rebuilds 15 of these remained in service until 1964/65. This line-up at King Street garage shows four of the AEC-powered CWA6s new in 1943/45, 144 (BRG 950) on the left with Brush body, 140/1/7 (BRG 916/7, BRS 29) bodied by Duple. All have grey roofs, a feature phased out from 1964. *Omnibus Society/Roy Marshall*

Duple-bodied CWA6 142 (BRG 935), new in June 1944, in Broad Street in February 1965, revealing the extent to which these buses were rebuilt in the late 1950s. It came out of service the following September. The Gothic-style granite building is Marischal College (pronounced Marshall) built in the 1830s as part of the university and since 2011 the headquarters of the city council. *W S Philip*

The first postwar AECs for Aberdeen were 10 Weymann-bodied Regent IIIs with London RT-type low-bonnet chassis, which entered service between December 1946 and March 1947. They were rebuilt in 1957/58 with remounted upper deck front windscreens, contemporary destination displays and with one additional seat downstairs and remained in service until 1966. This is 22 (BRS 522) in Broad Street in October 1965. *W S Philip*

Until the early 1950s, a darker shade of green was employed along with prominent fleetnames and fleet numbers, as on 47 (DRG 447), one of 10 Weymann-bodied AEC Regent IIIs new in 1949 and kept for 18 years; five similar buses were new in 1947. It is outside the Joint Station, as the city's railway station – built by the Caledonian and Great North of Scotland Railways – was known until 1952. This particular structure, completed in 1916, was constructed of locally quarried granite. *C Carter*

Local coachbuilder Walker supplied Aberdeen with single- and double-deck bodies from 1929 until 1948. The last of these were seven rear-entrance Daimler CVD6 single-deckers and the last of all, in November 1948, was 15 (DRG 115). All were rebuilt as one-man-operated forward-entrance buses in 1956, in which condition 15 was photographed operating a feeder service to the tram service before it closed in 1958. It was the only one of these not subject to even more radical reconstruction and was the first to be withdrawn, in 1966. *Phil Tatt/ Online Transport Archive*

Unable to obtain new coaches at a price it was prepared to pay, the corporation stripped down and completely rebuilt the original bodies of four of the Walker-bodied Daimlers in 1962/63, retaining 44 (CRS 834) until as late as 1971 as a 29-seater with space for wheelchairs. *John Kaye*

The other two single-deckers lost their Walker bodies in 1958, when Alexander fitted new coachwork combining features of its last production halfcab bodies of seven years earlier with some of those on contemporary underfloor-engined single-deckers. This is 11 (CRG 811), with 1947 chassis, operating a city tour. *Geoffrey Morant*

Like Glasgow and Dundee, Aberdeen bought early postwar double-deckers with Northern Coachbuilders bodies. All were Daimlers. The last 10 were Gardner-powered CVG6s new in 1951, including 165 (DRS 365) photographed on Regent Quay. The chassis gave at least 20 years' service but their composite bodies, some of the last built by Northern Coachbuilders when the firm was closing down, were scrapped after just nine. *Geoffrey Morant*

Northern Coachbuilders-bodied Daimler 72 (BRS 572) was one of 13 CVD6s new in 1947. It was eight years old when photographed at Bridge of Dee terminus alongside one of the last 20 new trams for the corporation, delivered in 1948 and scrapped when the system closed 10 years later. The bodies on the Daimlers probably condemned them to shorter lives than the utilities, as all were withdrawn by 1963.
Ray DeGroote/Online Transport Archive

GARTHDEE
1
SALE SHOP
DRS 367

PRIVATE
WORLD RECORD PAYOUT
£835,495 ON LITTLEWOODS
IN ONE WEEK
AUCHINYELL
2
88
226
DRS 358
JRG226

Ten CVG6s new in 1950 had Brockhouse bodies built in Clydebank on Park Royal frames. They were rebuilt in 1961 and fitted with four additional seats and kept for a further five years. This February 1966 photograph, taken three months before withdrawal, shows 37 (DRG 337) passing construction work in West North Street. *W S Philip*

Opposite, top The 10 Northern Coachbuilders-bodied CVG6s received new 8ft-wide Alexander bodies in 1960, similar to those on 45 new CVG6s delivered between 1961 and 1965. Like the two rebodied single-deckers, they presented a curious mix of styles – bodies with glass fibre mouldings and sliding cab doors, chassis with exposed radiators and front chassis members. This is 167 (DRS 367) before withdrawal in 1971. *Omnibus Society/Roy Marshall*

Opposite, lower A markedly more successful body purchase was of 15 from Weymann in 1950 on Daimler CVG6s, the first buses in the fleet with sliding cab doors. All gave at least 18 years' service and 88 (DRS 358), originally numbered 158, lasted until 1970. It was photographed at a popular spot for photographers, the Castle Street terminus at the eastern end of Union Street in the city centre, alongside 226 (JRG 226), a 1956 CVG6 with Metro-Cammell Orion body. Both demonstrate the final version of double-deck livery, with cream roof. *Omnibus Society/Roy Marshall*

The final phases of tram replacement helped bring the first 101 concealed radiator double-deckers into the fleet between 1954 and 1958, 71 Daimler CVG6s and 30 AEC Regent Vs with a mix of Metro-Cammell, Crossley and Park Royal bodies. This line-up at Castle Street shows Daimler 238 (KRG 236) new in 1957 and Crossley-bodied AEC 209 (HRG 209) of 1955 either side of 1945 Duple-bodied Daimler CWA6 151 (BRS 33), which was withdrawn in 1965. The AEC survives in preservation as a long-term restoration project. *Omnibus Society/Roy Marshall*

There were just five Crossley-bodied AEC Regent Vs, to the D2RV6G specification built only for Aberdeen and Glasgow with Gardner 6LW engines, vacuum brakes, spring-operated preselector gearboxes and pressed metal radiator grilles. The Aberdeen quintet had chassis numbers directly after Glasgow's 75. This is 208 (HRG 208) in June 1970, the year before withdrawal and the last year before decimal currency ended prices like two shillings and ninepence for the purchase of Twirl cooking oil. *Omnibus Society/ Roy Marshall*

Forty-five Daimler CVG6s new in 1954/55, including 201 (HRG 201), had Crossley bodies similar to those on the Gardner-powered Regents. It is next to a gas lamp in Gallowgate. *W S Philip*

Forty Daimlers new in 1954/55, including 200 (HRS 200) turning out of Guild Street close to the city's rail and bus stations, had Crossley bodies similar to those on the Gardner-powered Regents. It was withdrawn prematurely after an accident in 1968, the others surviving into the early 1970s. *Alan Mortimer*

The remaining 25 Regent Vs were supplied with AEC engines and Monocontrol semi-automatic gearboxes. Five in 1957, like 251 (KRS 251), had bodies by Park Royal, like Crossley and AEC part of the Associated Commercial Vehicles group. Upon withdrawal in 1973, all five were sold to Greyhound of Arbroath, which bought many surplus Aberdeen buses at the time. *Geoffrey Morant*

Metro-Cammell Orion bodies were specified on all 15 of the Regents delivered in 1958, including 256 (KRS 256), photographed on Union Bridge. The bus had had its first repaint, its front mudguards having been shortened to reduce risk of accident damage and improve airflow to the brakes. These buses replaced the last trams in May 1958 and survived into the first year of Grampian ownership. *Jim Thomson*

The last of the Regent Vs, new in June 1959, also were Aberdeen's first double-deckers bodied by Alexander, which was steadily dominating the Scottish municipal market. Tram tracks were still in place over a year after the last trams had been withdrawn as 272 (MRS 272) gleams fresh from the Falkirk coachworks. *Geoffrey Morant*

The five Alexander-bodied Regents had their AEC engines replaced with Gardner 6LWs in 1963, a conversion that required their radiators to be moved forward slightly to accommodate the longer engine – hence the grille and panel below standing proud of the rest of the bonnet assembly on 271 (MRS 271) in this September 1969 photograph in Justice Street. Under-canopy saloon heaters were also fitted when the engines were changed. All five were sold in 1976. *Omnibus Society/Roy Marshall*

The last Metro-Cammell Orion bodies to join the fleet arrived in 1960 on 12 Daimler CVG6s with the later Manchester-style bonnet assembly. Numerically at least, 287 (ORG 287) was the last of the batch, which were similar to a solitary bus new two years earlier. *Geoffrey Morant*

In West North Street in October 1962 is 291 (RRG 291) new in May 1961, from the first batch of the 45 Alexander-bodied CVG6s that would be Aberdeen's last new halfcabs. *W S Philip*

Between 1968 and 1971, eight Alexander-bodied CVG6s – one new in 1962, the others in 1964 – underwent a major conversion from rear to forward entrance for one-man operation, increasing their unladen weight by nearly a quarter of a ton and reducing the seating capacity by one. One-man halfcabs were never terribly satisfactory anywhere but despite that most outlasted the newer open-platform Daimlers, the last coming out of service in 1980. This is one of the 1964 buses, 323 (VRS 323), passing Aberdeen harbour on a city tour before oil industry vessels took the place of fishing trawlers. *Geoffrey Morant*

A nearside view of 321 (VRS 321), another of the rebuilt Daimlers, showing the angled bulkhead intended to facilitate fare collection by the driver. It is in King Street garage, next to the head office building completed and first occupied in 1862 by the Royal Aberdeenshire Highlanders. It was acquired by the corporation tramways department in 1914 but remained in military use until the end of World War 1 in 1918. *Omnibus Society/ Roy Marshall*

The final eight CVG6s arrived in 1965, like eight new the previous years fitted with the wider bonnet and grille by then standard for all front-engined Daimlers but originally only on 30ft models. This is 332 (CRG 332C), last of the batch and the last open rear platform bus for any Scottish municipal fleet. *Alan Mortimer*

Opposite, top The last new halfcab may have been delivered five years earlier, but in 1970 Aberdeen felt the need of a driver training bus with a manual gearbox. The solution came from Alexander (Midland) in the shape of 97 (DMS 351), a 1951 Leyland Titan PD2/12 with lowbridge version of the final design of Leyland bodywork, which was kept for four years. *John Kaye*

Opposite, lower Daimler held on to Aberdeen's business with its first rear-engined buses, 12 Alexander-bodied Fleetlines new in 1966. This is 108 (ERG 108D) heading east along Guild Street. *Geoffrey Morant*

MOUNTHOOLY
22
PRIVATE
97
174
GRG 174
L
DMS 351

STATION HOTEL
British SAVINGS BONDS
£5 units from Post Offices & Banks
9
GUILD STREET
108
ERG 108D

Other than a Titan TD1 demonstrator in 1930/1, the first Leylands ever for Aberdeen were 12 Tiger Cubs with dual-door Alexander Y-type bodies new in 1966/67, the first of a growing fleet of standee single-deckers for the conversion of routes to one-man operation. One of the six in service from June 1967, 8 (GRS 8E), shows their original livery with all lower panels painted cream. *Geoffrey Morant*

Presumably to disguise the worst effects of road dirt, single-deckers later gained green side skirts, as on 1 (ERG 1D) leaving Castle Street. *Omnibus Society/Roy Marshall*

With a change of general manager and no rear-engined double-deck offering available from AEC, Leyland secured its first double-deck order from Aberdeen to supply 10 Atlanteans in 1967. Like the Fleetlines, they had Alexander's A-type body and nine, including 115 (GRS 115E) were to the same style with standard length windows. One of these was later rebuilt with a centre door. *Alan Mortimer*

Its panoramic windows made 121 (GRS 121E), the last of the batch, odd one out among the Atlanteans. It is crossing from King Street into Marshall Street with the junction of Union Street/Castlegate behind. At the time of writing it was one of five buses carrying advertising for confectionery by J E Esselmont whose premises were at the south end of King Street a few yards to the left of 121. *Omnibus Society/Roy Marshall*

Three AEC Reliances with single-door 45-seat Alexander Y-type bodies followed in 1968 and 1970 for the city tour. Although fitted with bus seats, they were painted in coach livery of cream with green window surrounds and had illuminated house glasses above the front wheels, showing 'ACT'. This is one of the 1968 pair, 13 (LRG 13G). *Geoffrey Morant*

The rear-engined standee single-decker of choice, offering a lower floor in the front half, was the AEC Swift, of which 37 were bought between 1968 and 1972, all with Alexander W-type bodies with panoramic windows. Unlike contemporary purchases in Dundee and Glasgow, these were to the shorter 10m length, which may have caused fewer body problems than on 11m buses. Nevertheless, their lives were short by Aberdeen standards, all being withdrawn between 1979 and 1982. The first 10, used to convert the Kincorth Circular services to one-man operation, had MP2R chassis with low driving positions, a front end unique to the W-type and single-width centre exit doors. When new in June 1968, these buses – including 20 (JRS 20F) – were cream with green roof and side flashes beneath the shallower side windows towards the rear. *Alan Mortimer*

The 15 Swifts new in 1969, like 30 (NRG 30H) at Hazlehead, had 2MP2R chassis with a higher driving position. Accordingly, they had the same front-end design as contemporary Alexander Y-type bodies, as well as wider centre exits with four-leaf doors. This also shows the green skirts added to the livery of all the Swifts from 1972. Advertising appeared on the cover panels of single-deckers from 1970 to maintain commercial revenue in a fleet with fewer double-deckers. *Geoffrey Morant*

The 12 Swifts new in 1971 and 1972 had the later 'double grille' style of lower dash panel found on the Y-type. All front grilles on the Swift were entirely decorative, as the radiator was in the offside rear, beneath the emergency door on 50 (SRS 50K), which entered service in December 1971 and was sold in May 1982. This one saw further service on the southern outskirts of London, with Golden Miller of Feltham. *Geoffrey Morant*

For the first time since it had acquired 14 trams from Manchester in 1947/48, Aberdeen bought second-hand in May 1971 when it grasped the opportunity to take a quartet of seven-year-old AEC Reliances from Leeds City Transport. These Roe-bodied two-door 41-seaters with Monocontrol semi-automatic transmission had become surplus in a Leeds fleet awash with rear-engined Swifts and Fleetlines. By chance, their fleet and matching registration numbers – this is 47 (47 KUA) in Market Street – fitted in the Aberdeen series, starting just three places after the highest numbered Swifts then in service. *Omnibus Society/Peter Henson*

The gap between the fleet numbers of the 1969 Swifts and the ex-Leeds Reliances was filled by three 10.3m Leyland Nationals delivered in February 1973. These were the 137th, 138th and 139th production Leyland Nationals built and their arrival quadrupled the population of the type in Scotland, where a solitary example with AA Motor Services in Ayrshire (the 56th production bus) was as far as this mass produced vehicle had got against the Scottish Bus Group's steadfast resistance to Leyland's sales efforts. More followed after Grampian had taken over, but these three were scrapped in 1979. This is first of the trio 41 (VRS 41L) in Union Street. *Omnibus Society/Roy Marshall*

The first double-deckers in four years also were the first Daimlers for five years. These 80-seaters new at the beginning of 1971, inevitably dubbed 'jumbos' so soon after Boeing had changed the size and shape of air travel, were 33ft (10m) two-door vehicles with Alexander L-type bodies for the 'Bridges' route linking the Bridges of Don to the north of the city and Dee to the south. They were the first double-deckers delivered already equipped for one-man operation and the only ones supplied with centre rather than forward staircases. They somehow seemed apt successors to the 20 centre-door 76-seat trams that served the route from 1949 to 1958. This is 133 (PRG 133J) in Union Street after the construction of shops on the previously open south side of Union Bridge. *Geoffrey Morant*

Nearside view of 'jumbo' Fleetline 134 (PRG 134J) at the eastern end of Union Street after Autofare cash vaults were introduced from 1973. The last of these buses were withdrawn in 1982, though many saw further service with other operators. Today, First operates high-capacity articulated Volvo 'bendybuses' on the Bridges routes. *Geoffrey Morant*

There was a two-year gap before the next 12 double-deckers, Aberdeen's last Fleetlines and after 37 years its last Daimlers, arrived in 1973. These had Leyland 680 rather than Gardner 6LX engines and reverted to the shorter length of the 1966/67 double-deckers. Their 74-seat Alexander AL-type bodies followed the layout of two-door double-deckers in the other Scottish city fleets, with a forward ascending staircase over the offside front wheel and the centre door directly behind the nearside front wheel. This layout placed the exit closer to drivers' sightline and farther away from the danger to alighting passengers of the rear wheels. Seven of them, including 144 (VRS 144L), were sold to Scottish Bus Group companies in 1983. *Geoffrey Morant*

The Leyland Atlantean AN68 became the standard double-decker from November 1973 until Grampian took delivery of the last of 189 in March 1983 – the highest level of standardisation that the fleet ever achieved in municipal ownership. All had Alexander AL-type bodies similar to those on the 1973 Fleetlines. Among the first to arrive was 156 (NRG 156M) photographed in Guild Street. *Omnibus Society/Roy Marshall*

Added to the fleet in November 1974 for a new suburban route was 60 (GSA 860N), the prototype Alexander S-type midibus, a 27-seat integral based on Ford A-Series light truck running units. Alexander had exhibited it at the Commercial Motor Show in London that September, painted in Edinburgh Corporation madder and white. Although painted in Aberdeen colours, it was on extended loan from Alexander, to whom it returned during 1976 when Grampian received three production vehicles, with restyled body. *Omnibus Society/ Peter Henson*

The final additions, in the last month of Aberdeen Corporation's existence in April 1975, were six 1959 Alexander-bodied Daimler CVG6s from Greater Glasgow PTE. They were among the first vehicles in the green, cream and orange of Grampian, with whom they entered service in May and July along with two others that arrived in July 1975. Most were kept little more than a year, including 341 (SGD241), originally Glasgow D258. *Geoffrey Morant*

Dundee

For much of the period covered in this book, Dundee's buses were more workaday than elegant. Varied, interesting and sometimes unusual, but betraying less overt civic pride than their counterparts in Edinburgh, Aberdeen or Glasgow.

Perhaps this reflects the character of this small hilly city honed by its industries and location where the Firth of Tay meets the North Sea.

As in the other three cities, the tram was king, but Dundee also was a pioneer of the trolleybus, a pair of which operated from 1912 to 1914 along an unsurfaced Clepington Road on the northern edge of town, connecting two radial routes. The toxic combination of solid tyres and rough roadway did for them rather than their electric propulsion. Contemporary motorbuses would have fared no better.

Motorbuses came to stay in 1921 and the operation grew to serve new housing. The last new trams arrived in 1930, and although most of the network remained intact until 1953 it then sneaked in a month ahead of Edinburgh to be the first to abandon them completely in October 1956.

They might have lasted longer had it not been for some over-optimistic forecasting 400 miles away, where London Transport found itself with more vehicles than it needed at a time when the car was beginning to erode public transport patronage. Presented with the chance to purchase 40 surplus AEC Regents – including a quarter of the non-standard Cravens RTs – it brought forward the shutdown that had only begun in earnest 11 months before.

By the 1960s, the city's gritty industrial relations were impacting on the bus service, with titanic tussles between management and unions over the first moves towards one-man operation in which its first 36ft single-deckers were a particular bone of contention. As in Glasgow, there was serious talk of offloading the service to the still profitable Scottish Bus Group.

The appearance of the fleet seemed to track the decline in the organisation's finances and sense of self-worth. Originally blue and white, the livery had been green and white since 1934 when a change of general manager saw the departing one take blue to his new posting in Hull. Big, bold and proud fleetnames disappeared and steadily the proportion of white decreased to the point in 1964 when the first rear-engined double-deckers arrived in all over green. Arguably, the look got even worse when an even darker shade was added as a second colour to distinguish vehicles operated without a conductor.

In its last months, as it was made ready for transfer to Tayside Region in May 1975 and the new council's director of public transport acted as general manager, a handful of older buses was brightened by a decent area of white relief. Tayside brightened things even more by adopting blue once again as the colour – two tones separated by white – in one of the most radical livery transformations of that decade.

Like Aberdeen, Dundee's purchasing policy was to favour AEC and Daimler from 1935, though Daimler was sole provider of double-deckers after 1953. Consequently, unlike Aberdeen or Glasgow it bought no Regent Vs and with a predominantly double-deck fleet only 20 more AECs arrived new after 1954, Reliances in 1965/66 and Swifts in 1968. However, a policy of retaining its buses longer than the other cities ensured that its last Regent IIIs were still (just) active when Tayside took over.

Sold to management and employees in 1991, the successor undertaking today is part of National Express, an offshoot of its huge West Midlands bus division and the group's only business north of the border. The livery became green once more in 2015.

Opposite, top Sixteen utility Daimler CWA6s were delivered between 1943 and 1945 and, following extensive body modernisation, remained in the fleet until 1965. This May 1955 view at Maryfield garage shows two of them in substantially original condition. Northern Counties-bodied 88 (YJ 7977) on the left was new in July 1944 as No.23, while the bus on the right is Duple-bodied 89 (YJ 7980), new in October 1944 as No.24. Tram No.55 in between was then around 30 years old. *Ray DeGroote/ Online Transport Archive*

Opposite, lower The utility Daimlers survived into an age of such 1960s British cars as the MkI Ford Cortina, the Hillman Imp and BMC 1100. This is heavily rebuilt Northern Counties-bodied 92 (YJ 7983), new in June 1944 as No.27, in the High Street in June 1964. *Omnibus Society/Roy Marshall*

SPACE PILOTS TRAIN ON
THORNWOOD
MACAROON BARS 3d
D
No88
YJ7997

RESTAURANT
KEILLER
20
GO TO TOWN WITH Crown WALLPAPERS
YJ7983

Twenty Northern Coachbuilders-bodied Daimler CVD6s delivered in 1947 formed the largest intake of new buses to Dundee since it began bus operations 26 years earlier. They gave between 19 and 20 years' passenger service. This 1962 photograph at Marchbanks garage shows 35 (YJ 9039) alongside 112 (YJ 8105), one of three Daimler CWD6s with Duple relaxed utility bodies new in May 1946 and heavily rebuilt around 1958/59. *Iain MacGregor*

An early postwar bus to have a long afterlife as an ancillary vehicle was 4 (YJ 9127), one of five rear-entrance Weymann-bodied Daimler CVD6s new in 1947/48. Most were kept in service until 1965 when this one became a trainer. In 1971 it transferred to the corporation's social work department to carry disabled people and was rescued for an eventually abandoned preservation project in 1980. *Geoffrey Morant*

The first postwar AECs were 10 Regent IIIs new in the latter part of 1948 with Metro-Cammell bodies similar to contemporary vehicles for Glasgow. This is 58 (YJ 9131) at Maryfield garage, with first of batch 55 (YJ 9128) behind; 58 was one of the last withdrawn in 1968. *J G Todd/ Online Transport Archive*

Nineteen double-deckers new in 1949/50 were bodied in Norwich by Barnard, which made a short-lived move into the bus market, having recruited Northern Coachbuilders' chief engineer and senior draughtsman when they resigned from the former firm in 1948. Not surprisingly, the Barnard bodies had an NCB-look. First to arrive were 10 Daimler CVD6s, including 115 (ATS 905) photographed at the corporation's Dock Street city centre bus station in its original livery with cream roof, gold lining and large fleetnames discontinued to make way for commercial advertising. These bodies were scrapped after just 10 years. *C Carter*

The nine Barnard-bodied AEC Regent IIIs had a raked front more like the Metro-Cammell buses new in 1948. They were kept in passenger service until 1969/70 and 143 (AYJ 373), photographed close to the spot where Daimler 115 was photographed when new, lasted a further three years as a driver trainer. Green with a single white band became the standard livery from 1961. *Geoffrey Morant*

The Barnard-bodied Daimlers received new Alexander bodies in 1959/60, action that kept all of them in service until 1972, and four at least two years longer. While Alexander's standard body – even the 10 Daimlers rebodied around the same time for Aberdeen – were of four-bay design, these retained the five bay layout of the original Barnard structure, making them quite different from any other product of the Falkirk factory. This is 118 (ATS 908), with a Bundy timing clock behind, next to a bus shelter. *Geoffrey Morant*

Of the 65 Brockhouse bodies built for the four Scottish municipals, the fewest – just three – went to Dundee in September 1950 on AEC Regent IIIs, which gave 20 years' passenger service. The original plan was for these bodies to go on three Regents new in 1932. As with so many types in this fleet, the long working life made it likely that these were the last working examples of the Clydebank factory, which used Park Royal framing. This picture of 147 (BTS 117) was taken in 1964. *Omnibus Society/Roy Marshall*

The last 7ft 6in-wide double-deckers were 10 Daimler CVD6s with bodies built in Glasgow by Croft Bodybuilding and Engineering, new in 1950/51 and kept in passenger service until 1970-72. Here, driver and conductress converse in front of 132 (BTS 472). Similar 127, painted in the early postwar livery, is preserved as part of a collection for a new Museum of Transport that opened in the city in 2014. *Omnibus Society/Peter Henson*

The final halfcab single-deckers also were Dundee's first long wheelbase motorbuses. These 10 Daimler CVD6s, new in spring 1951, had 39-seat rear-entrance Brush bodies and most were kept until decidedly less robust AEC Swifts replaced them in 1968. Four years earlier, 17 (BTS 497) and 8 (BTS 488) still wore the single-deck version of pre-1961 livery with white window surrounds and orange lining out. *Omnibus Society/Roy Marshall*

Opposite, top Dundee's last new exposed radiator buses, which also were its first built to 8ft width, arrived in 1953. There were 10 Daimler CVD6s with Weymann bodies, four of which survived until 1975 when they were the last exposed radiator Daimlers left in any of the four city fleets. Like so many of the undertaking's buses bought up to this time, they lost some of their original appearance with the installation of replacement rubber-mounted glazing upon overhaul. The 'M' above the driver's windscreen indicates that 77 (CTS 636) was allocated to Maryfield garage when photographed in 1970. *Omnibus Society/Roy Marshall*

Opposite, lower The other seven new double-deckers in 1953 were the city's first with Alexander bodies and also its last new AEC double-deckers. These were among 29 Regent IIIs bought between 1948 and 1953, against 50 double-deck and 15 single-deck Daimler CVD6s new since 1947. Most, including 136 (CYJ 251), came out of service in 1974, but two lasted into 1975. *Geoffrey Morant*

SEAGATE
LICENSED
BETTING
OFFICE
AND
do it yourself supermar
REFUGE ASSURANCE Co Ltd
CITY CENTRE
35
77
CTS 636
HOUSEHOLD SUPPLIES Co Ltd

REFUGE ASSURANCE Co Ltd
PICCADILLY
Britain's finest cigarette.
MENZIESHILL
22
ITY CENTRE
136
CYJ 251

Like Glasgow and Edinburgh, Dundee bought heavyweight first generation underfloor-engined single-deckers, favouring AEC's Regal IV with an order for five, four of which arrived in spring 1953. This quartet all had 44-seat Weymann bodies and although crew-operated when new they were adapted for one-man operation in 1970/71, towards the end of their lives when newer buses had blazed the trail for the difficult phasing out of conductors in a city where industrial relations often were confrontational. When new, a waistband and the panels above the side windows were white, with Corporation Transport in capital letters on the waistbands. Turning from Pitfour Street to climb City Road is 19 (CTS 528) in the livery applied before 1961.
J G Todd/Online Transport Archive

As early as 1956, Regal IV 20 (CTS 529) was converted to 40-seat dual door layout as part of an unsuccessful attempt to experiment with one-man operation. This view at the junction of Commercial Street and the Seagate in the city centre was taken in 1970, four years before it was withdrawn and converted back to single-door layout for use by another council department. 'N' identified buses based at Marchbanks garage.
Omnibus Society/Roy Marshall

The fifth Regal IV, 22 (CYJ 315), arrived in 1954 and was Dundee's first Alexander-bodied single-decker. The styling of the 39-seat dual-door body was unique to this vehicle, similar but by no means identical to one on an early Leyland Tiger Cub demonstrator. When new, it had an American farebox and operated a peak hour express service at a premium fare, but there was no agreement for it to run without a conductor and the experiment was short lived. It saw limited use for many years after that, like the other Regals often being used for private hires, but nonetheless survived until 1974. *Campbell Sayers*

After the modest purchases of the early 1950s, replacement of the tram service saw a rapid increase in new double-deck deliveries, with 71 new Daimler CVG6s delivered between 1955 and 1957. They also brought Birmingham-style concealed radiators and full-width bonnets into the fleet for the first time, as well as lightweight bodywork, mainly of the Metro-Cammell Weymann organisation's Orion design also favoured by Edinburgh and Aberdeen. There were 65 Orions, 35 built by Metro-Cammell and 30 by Weymann. Heeling over dramatically on the Pitfour Street/City Road junction is Weymann-bodied 259 (FYJ 799) of the 1957 delivery in its original paint scheme. *J G Todd/Online Transport Archive*

RSMcC
A good name to protect your home with
GRE
Guardian Royal Exchange Assurance
DUPLICATE
22
ETS 979
BURT

The Royal Bank of Scotland
FINTRY
32
CARRY HOME Carlsberg SPECIAL BREW
SPECIAL BREW
40
FTS 214
BUS STOP

The availability of 40 surplus London Transport AEC Regents in 1956 hastened the end of the trams. Thirty amounted to one quarter of the 120 non-standard RTs with five-bay Cravens bodies new in 1949/50. They lasted more then 12 years and appear to have been numbered in the order in which they arrived, with a seemingly random mix of JXC and KGK registrations. They retained their London 'top box' route number displays, with the ultimate destination in a reduced version of its original position. This shows the livery into which they were first painted in Dundee on 234 (JXC 196), the former RT1433. *Geoffrey Morant*

Opposite, top The 35 CVG6s with Metro-Cammell bodies delivered in 1955 included 199 (ETS 979) in the post-1961 livery and displaying a destination informative only to those with an intimate knowledge of where a 22 might run. *Geoffrey Morant*

Opposite, lower The oddities among these 'tin front' Daimlers were six with four-bay Park Royal bodies delivered in June 1956. They were the only Park Royal bodies that Dundee bought postwar and its first since five AEC and Daimler double-deckers arrived in the early 1930s. Non-standard they may have been, but they led lives as long as those of the Orions. *Geoffrey Morant*

Post-1961 livery on Cravens-bodied 219 (KGK 732), originally London Transport RT1473. *Jim Thomson*

Along with the RTs came 10 Weymann-bodied Regent IIs new in 1945/46, half of the final and only post-war batch of STL-class double-deckers in London Transport's Country Area. They lasted eight years in Dundee, where they were latterly the only manual gearbox buses in the fleet. This August 1963 photograph shows 179 (HGC 232) which was STL2699 in London. *Michael Russell*

Ten more Metro-Cammell Orion-bodied Daimler CVG6s – the last before a change to sourcing all new bodies from Alexander – entered service in August 1958. They were the first for Dundee with the glass fibre bonnet assembly developed originally for Manchester. This is 271 (HTS 271), numerically the first of the batch. *Geoffrey Morant*

The last seven halfcab double-deckers bought new were Alexander-bodied Daimler CVG6s in 1960, with a design of front roof dome and wide dividing pillar between the top deck windscreens that somehow lacked the balanced proportions of similar bodies built for the other three cities. Like all of Dundee's Daimlers, these had preselector gearboxes. Bus 104 (KTS 96) was originally No.96, but along with three others was renumbered to make way for the first Daimler Fleetlines. *Geoffrey Morant*

Given that Daimler had supplied all 88 of Dundee's new front-engined double-deckers between 1955 and 1960, it was perhaps no huge surprise that its first rear-engined examples were the same manufacturer's Fleetline, although it tried Fleetline and Leyland Atlantean demonstrators before placing its initial order for 20 delivered in 1964. A further 45 followed in 1966 and 1968/69. These took livery simplification to its ultimate conclusion, the curves of their Alexander bodies devoid of any relief colour save their advertisement panels, as on this 1970 view of 99 (AYJ 99B) from the original batch. It is in the main garage at Dock Street to which all operations transferred. *John Kaye*

If a batch of buses tells a story, then it is the 10 AEC Reliances with 51-seat Alexander Y-type bodies ordered in 1961, bodied in 1964 and not delivered until 1966. These were Dundee's first 36ft single-deckers, intended to begin a conversion of routes to one-man operation. A lengthy dispute between management and union left them stored at the bodybuilder's for over a year and when delivered they were initially restricted to works and schools services. They were unique among Y-types in having Dundee's two-line destination box, an arrangement achieved with a moulding resembling an over-size cash register. Combined with its original unrelieved green livery, 26 (CTS 126D) presents a distinctly utilitarian appearance. *Omnibus Society/Peter Henson*

The later livery, intended to identify one-man buses, with dark green relief applied to Reliance 34 (CTS 134D). Long before Lancaster and other operators demanded it on their Y-types, Dundee specified wide entrances and four-leaf doors to try and reduce the time these high-floor buses spent at stops. *Geoffrey Morant*

The last new AECs were 10 rear-engined 36ft Swifts with Alexander W-type bodies delivered in 1968. Their dual-door layout accommodated 49 seats with relatively narrow front and centre doors and, as evident on 58 (GYJ 458G) in 1970, their livery was brightened by a return of white relief around the waistband. Swifts later became two-tone green. These buses also were caught up in fraught industrial relations, placed in service with conductors before a single-manning agreement was struck. *John Kaye*

Four more Swifts were acquired second hand from the Lanarkshire independent, Hutchison of Overtown, which preferred its standard choice of the mid-engined Reliance. Two, including 65 (NVD 310F), had 51-seat single-door W-type bodies otherwise similar to the 10 new to Dundee. They were acquired in 1971 and entered service in two-tone green. *Geoffrey Morant*

Opposite, top The other two ex-Hutchison Swifts had Willowbrook bodies, the only examples that Dundee ever owned. They were acquired in 1972. Look through the driver's windscreen of 68 (NVD 315F) and a folded baby buggy is in the nearside luggage rack behind the entrance, a reminder of the days before the low-floor accessibility revolution of the 1990s. *Omnibus Society/Peter Henson*

Opposite, lower The first buses painted two-tone green were 25 single-deck Daimler Fleetlines with Alexander W-type bodies new in 1970. Like other Fleetline customers, Dundee was attracted by once again being able to buy single- and double-deckers with largely the same chassis. It would come to rue the decision, as the big Gardner engine and long rear overhang combined with the weakness of the body around the centre door to begin tearing these buses apart by the time they were seven years old. All underwent various forms of rebuilding and four eventually were rebodied. All this is in the future and something for Tayside to address as second-of-batch 212 (KTS 212H) prepares to turn right near the ramps leading from the Tay Road Bridge in corporation days. *Omnibus Society/Peter Henson*

N
BARNHILL (Balmossie)
10
68
PAY AS YOU ENTER
NVD 315F

CIRCULAR
7
212
PAY AS YOU ENTER
KTS 212H

Double-deckers were back in favour for Dundee's final purchases, of 40 Fleetlines in 1972 and 1975. These were all 83-seat 33ft models with Alexander AL-type bodies incorporating peaked roof domes and flat windscreens. As is evident on 147 (PYJ 447L) from the earlier delivery of 25, Autofare cash vaults had ended the practice of drivers giving change and destination displays on double-deckers were single-line like those on the W-type single-deckers. These would be the last Fleetlines for the undertaking but they set a pattern that Tayside would follow of specifying high capacity long double-deckers. *Geoffrey Morant*

A cross-section of the Dundee fleet in Dock Street garage shortly before the undertaking passed to Tayside. A Weymann Orion-bodied Daimler CVG6 is on the left, two Alexander-bodied Daimler Fleetlines in two-tone green are on the right, with 1953 AEC Regent IIIs and Daimler CVD6s laid up at the back of the yard. *Omnibus Society/Roy Marshall*

With new bus deliveries running late and the oldest municipal fleet in Scotland, Dundee once again bought second hand in the weeks leading up to the transition to Tayside ownership in 1975. Surprise purchases for a fleet of AECs and Daimlers with semi-automatic or preselector gearboxes were 15 manual gearbox Leyland Titan PD2/20s with Metro-Cammell Orion bodies from Edinburgh. These were barely newer than Dundee's oldest CVD6s and Regent IIIs, as they dated from between 1954 and 1956. Edinburgh repainted them, mostly in Tayside blue and white, but the first few came in this final version of Dundee livery, with white lower deck window surrounds, a style also applied to a few of the 1958 Daimlers. A gleaming 4 (LFS 488) has had a Tayside crest applied above the cab door. *Omnibus Society/Peter Henson*

Tayside's first director of public transport, Alan Westwell, had been chief engineer at Glasgow Corporation and Greater Glasgow PTE before taking up his new post and in April 1975 arranged for Dundee Corporation to acquire eight Alexander-bodied Daimler CVG6s from the PTE in April 1975 to strip for spare parts. One, former Glasgow D183 (SGD 167), was considered good enough to keep as a driver trainer, numbered T2, and was painted in a variation of the new council's two-tone blue and white Tayside livery. This line-up at Dock Street garage shows it between two AEC single-deckers in the new colours, Reliance 25 (CTS 125D) and Swift 57 (GYJ 457G). T2 was kept until the end of 1977. *Alan Millar*

Company operators

The corporation fleets may have dominated the four major cities, but they did not have the streets to themselves.

The companies of the state-owned Scottish Bus Group – each one with its own distinctive livery – operated extensively into and around Glasgow, Edinburgh, Aberdeen and Dundee with a mix of interurban and local services.

As 'country' buses, higher fares helped steer passengers towards the municipals for local journeys and in Glasgow an Act of Parliament prevented operators other than the corporation from carrying passengers making journeys entirely within the city boundaries as they had applied at the start of this arrangement in 1930.

In Perth, which regained city status in 2012 after losing it in 1975, company buses ran with a municipal twist. Perth Corporation operated trams from 1903 to 1929, then a small fleet of buses until Alexander's – part of the Scottish Motor Traction group that later became SBG – took over in 1934 on a 21-year lease. Most Alexander's buses then were blue, but the Perth city fleet was dark red until 1962.

Nor were all companies owned by SBG. Glasgow also was home to MacBrayne's, neither independent nor part of SBG, with its highly colourful fleet operating daily services to the West Highlands until its bus operations passed to SBG in 1970.

Independents operated into the heart of Aberdeen until the mid-1960s, to Dundee for all the years covered by this book and over the same period into parts of Glasgow and extensively in adjoining Paisley.

Alexander's E18 (FWG 853), a 1955 ECW-bodied Bristol LS6G, departing Dundas Street Bus Station, Glasgow, for Leven in Fife, with a red David Lawson's Bristol Lodekka on the left of the picture and a pre-war Leyland Tiger behind the LS. The correct route number for the Leven service was 27 and not the 270 set by the LS's crew. *Jim Thomson*

Scottish Bus Group

Alexander's red and blue buses in Perth. RO530 (AMS 276), a 1945 Northern Counties-bodied Guy Arab II in the dark red livery used for former corporation routes, stands between a pair of the company's blue 'country' buses. A7 (AMS 587) on its left is a 1948 Burlingham-bodied AEC Regal and P707 (WG 3250) is a 1935 Alexander-bodied Leyland Lion LT5A. *Alan B Cross*

Besides wartime Guy Arabs operated since new, Alexander's ran ex-London Transport examples on Perth city services. RO701 (GYL 434) is an Arab II with Northern Counties relaxed utility body new in December 1945 as LT's G294. It is in Mill Street on a route serving the Muirton housing scheme to the north of the city. *Geoffrey Morant*

When the huge Alexander company was split three ways in 1961, the operations stretching between Perth and Glasgow went to the new Alexander (Midland) fleet, which retained the old company's blue and cream colours for all its activities. New 70-seat Bristol Lodekka FLF6Gs with forward entrances, flat floors and saloon heating replaced the red utility Guys in 1962/63, by which time buses operating into Perth from Fife were starting to be painted red. This 1969 view of MRD172 (TWG 551) shows the script-style Midland fleetname introduced from 1962 but by then superseded by more modern typography. The Fife, Midland and Northern companies applied F, M or N prefixes to existing Alexander fleet numbers in 1961 and stuck to the same type codes as each other for the next 20 years. *Geoffrey Morant*

Operating a local service from Glasgow's north-eastern suburbs is Alexander (Midland) MRB247 (RMS 679), a lowbridge Alexander-bodied Leyland Titan PD3/3C. There were 17 of these in the fleet, built in 1961 with new chassis frames and bodies but running units transplanted from 10-year-old low mileage Tiger OPS2 coaches, which in turn received the guts of some older Tiger PS1s. The open space on the left would soon be filled with the inner city section of the M8 motorway. *Iain MacGregor*

Emerging through the arches of Edinburgh's April 1957 bus station at St Andrew Square in October 1968 is Alexander (Fife) FGA7 (GMS 417), a 1955 Alexander-bodied Guy Arab LUF downgraded from coach to bus livery. Fife began operating into Edinburgh when the Forth Road Bridge opened in September 1964 and FGA7, one of 20 similar vehicles new in 1955 and 1957, was based in Dunfermline, a few miles north of the suspension bridge. Eastern Scottish AEC and Bristol single-deckers may be glimpsed behind the Guy. *Geoffrey Morant*

The dark red livery also identified the fleet of Alexander's David Lawson subsidiary, based at Kirkintilloch and operating frequent services into Dundas Street bus station in Glasgow. RO458 (AMS 46) was a 1944 Guy Arab II rebodied by Eastern Coach Works in 1951, one of five in the fleet and among the first ECW bodies built for Scotland. Lawson's was absorbed into Alexander (Midland) when Alexander's was divided into three companies in 1961 and its buses were repainted blue. The single-decker is an Alexander-bodied Leyland Tiger Cub of Alexander (Fife), which adopted Ayres red – a lighter shade than the discontinued dark red – after the 1961 divide. *Campbell Sayers*

Alexander (Midland) bought 85 Daimler Fleetlines with lowheight Alexander bodywork between 1967 and 1970, of which MRF47 (MWG 779F) arrived in June 1968. This photograph from September 1969 shows it arriving in Glasgow, from Stirling via what the destination describes as Cumbernauld New Town, into a part of the city in the process of radical redevelopment. This is Parliamentary Road, a major thoroughfare that no longer exists today, where high-rise flats point into the sky as buses and buttoned-up pedestrians pass a wooden roadblock and rubble from property that has been demolished. The tenements, public bar and industrial sites would soon disappear. The Fleetline is following one of Midland's Alexander-bodied Albion Nimbus coaches. *Omnibus Society/Roy Marshall*

Prototype Ailsa double-decker THS 273M, with front-mounted Volvo engine and front-entrance Alexander body, was exhibited at the Scottish Motor Show in Glasgow in November 1973 in Midland livery and entered public service for the first time early in 1974 from the company's Milngavie depot, operating with driver and conductor on a busy commuter route between Glasgow city centre and Duntocher. There were limits to how many SBG depots and routes could accommodate the highbridge Ailsa, though Midland bought 14 in 1977 for Perth city services. In 1973, the Ailsa Bus head office was in Barrhead, hence the Renfrewshire registration of this pioneering vehicle, which SBG never owned but retained Midland colours when demonstrated to various potential customers in the UK and Ireland. It was shipped to Bangkok for further demonstration before being sold to Citybus in Hong Kong.
Geoffrey Morant

Alexander (Northern), which operated frequent services into Aberdeen, Dundee and Perth, adopted a stunning yellow and cream livery in place of blue. This September 1968 view shows ND20 (BMS 415), a 1948 Burlingham-bodied Daimler CVD6, leaving Aberdeen bus station for the hamlet of Cookney, around 10 miles to the south. Passengers awaiting corporation buses are standing at the red bus stop behind. *Geoffrey Morant*

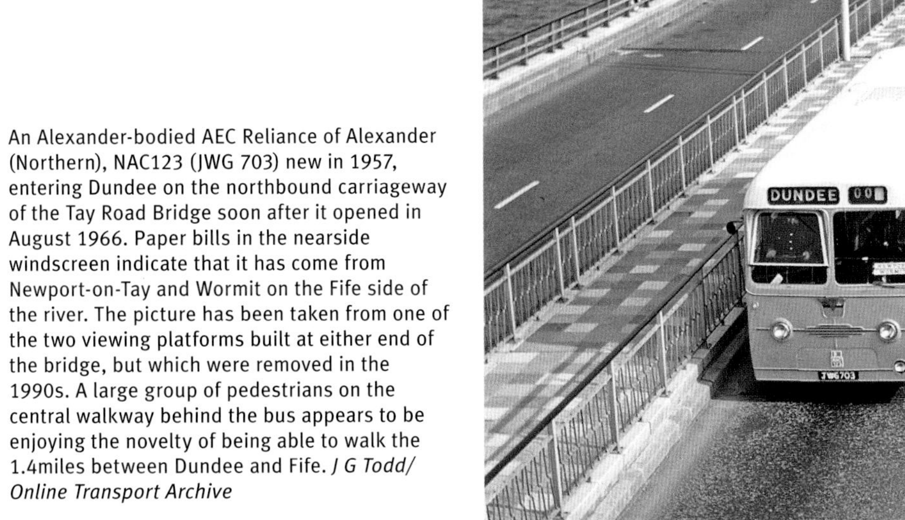

An Alexander-bodied AEC Reliance of Alexander (Northern), NAC123 (JWG 703) new in 1957, entering Dundee on the northbound carriageway of the Tay Road Bridge soon after it opened in August 1966. Paper bills in the nearside windscreen indicate that it has come from Newport-on-Tay and Wormit on the Fife side of the river. The picture has been taken from one of the two viewing platforms built at either end of the bridge, but which were removed in the 1990s. A large group of pedestrians on the central walkway behind the bus appears to be enjoying the novelty of being able to walk the 1.4miles between Dundee and Fife. *J G Todd/ Online Transport Archive*

Central SMT, based in Motherwell, operated an extensive network of services in Lanarkshire and Dunbartonshire, many of them into Glasgow. It served four main corridors between the city and Lanarkshire towns, numbered in the 40s, 50s, 60s and 70s. The 60 group combined to operate a high frequency service between Glasgow, Cambuslang and Hamilton before fanning out to their final destinations. A group of women, one of them with a hefty shopping bag, board one of the company's first postwar double-deckers, Northern Counties-bodied Leyland Titan PD1 L222 (BVD 911) new in August 1946, on the 62 to Fairhill, a new community built in the 1950s and 1960s to the south of Hamilton. *Omnibus Society/ Roy Marshall*

Central SMT B21 (GM 7021), a 1955 Bristol Lodekka LD6G with platform doors and 56 high-backed seats in its ECW body, is leaving Waterloo Street bus station close to Glasgow Central railway station at the start of the long route to Peebles in the Scottish Borders. This operated on a limited stop basis on sections shared with more frequent services between Glasgow, Wishaw and Lanark on the 40 group corridor between Glasgow and Bellshill. When new, B21 carried the mainly red livery shown on L222, but was repainted into this revised style with cream window surrounds first applied to new double-deckers delivered in 1956. Until 1953, Central buses had VA or VD registrations for Lanarkshire, but a boundary change took its head office into the Burgh of Motherwell & Wishaw, whose GM marks were issued until the vehicle registration system changed in 1974. *Campbell Sayers*

Although it bought Lodekkas from 1955, Central SMT continued taking lowbridge Leyland double-deckers until 1960. This highly profitable company was fastidious in controlling costs, buying Titan PD1s as late as 1952 and large numbers of 27ft double-deckers until 1964. L592 (GM 8832), photographed in Glasgow's George Square in June 1959 on a route to the new town of East Kilbride, was one of only 10 Titan PD3/3s purchased in 1957, its first 30ft double-deckers. Their 67-seat Northern Counties bodies held eight more passengers than contemporary PD2s, but the company calculated that this did not compensate for the additional purchase price, fuel consumption and fare-collection responsibility placed on conductors. *Geoffrey Morant*

Four Scottish Bus Group subsidiaries bought 109 early production Bristol VRTs between 1968 and early 1970, but disposed of them all – mainly to the National Bus Company in exchange for Lodekka FLFs – by 1974. They arrived just after SBG was separated from the state-owned undertakings in England and Wales, which held the state's shareholding in Bristol and Eastern Coach Works, and their considerable teething troubles presented SBG with an opportunity to exercise its new right not to buy Bristol products and indeed rid itself of what it regarded as a turbulent beast. All had ECW bodies and Central BN357 (NGM 157G) was numerically the first of 20 used mainly on one-man-operated local routes in Dumbarton and Motherwell & Wishaw, although they strayed occasionally into Glasgow. This is Dumbarton High Street in May 1972, nine months before BN357 departed for a new and long life with Eastern Counties. Following NBC's break-up of that company in September 1984, it passed to the new Cambus fleet and finally came out of service the following February. *Geoffrey Morant*

Scottish Omnibuses, which traded as Eastern Scottish from 1964, had its headquarters in Edinburgh and a territory stretching from Glasgow to Berwick-upon-Tweed. This is Edinburgh and H3 (SS 7525), an Alexander-bodied Leyland Tiger PS1 new to Stark's of Dunbar, whose business was acquired in 1964. Like many of Stark's buses, this had been built as an extra on a batch built at the same time for Alexander's. *Campbell Sayers*

Scottish Omnibuses continued to use the SMT name and diamond logo from pre-1949 private sector days, but between 1962 and 1964 changed this to 'Scottish' before adopting the geographically more precise Eastern Scottish from 1964. The 'Scottish' name appears in gold beneath the centre lower saloon window of BB93 (GSF 676), a Burlingham-bodied AEC Regent III new in 1950 and kept until 1967. The glazed upper deck ceiling panels are apparent in this August 1964 picture as it sets out from Edinburgh bus station for Gullane on the East Lothian coast with a standing load. Scottish Omnibuses used this light green and cream livery from 1952 to 1964 when it adopted the darker shade in the previous picture. *Omnibus Society/Roy Marshall*

The peak summer months frequently found Scottish Omnibuses short of vehicles, leading to colourful scenes in Edinburgh's St Andrew Square bus station such as this in the summer of 1963. The company had acquired Baxter's of Airdrie the previous December and one of its newest double-deckers, AEC/Park Royal Bridgemaster 78 (78 BVD) was operating 'on hire' on a route to East Lothian. The red double-decker is one of nine wartime Guy Arabs transferred from Highland Omnibuses in Inverness and press ganged into service for the summer. The green double-deckers (a Burlingham-bodied AEC Regent and a Bristol Lodekka) were in the main fleet. *Ian Dunnett/ Online Transport Archive*

When it was an independent company, Stark's buses carried the same SMT fleetnames as Scottish Omnibuses, but the Stark's name was applied after the 1964 takeover along with a lighter shade of green than the main fleet. This followed the decision the previous year to revive and retain the Baxter's identity in Airdrie and Coatbridge. Burlingham-bodied AEC Reliance B25 (UVA 115) straddles all of this story, as it was new to Baxter's and had become a Stark's bus by June 1973 as it led an Eastern Scottish-liveried Bristol Lodekka into Edinburgh bus station. The buses are in Leopold Place on London Road. *Omnibus Society/Roy Marshall*

191
DRUMPARK
OWS 552

COATBRIDGE
217
EASTERN SCOTTISH
B690H
SWS 690

MacBrayne's 189 (391 FGB), a 1962 AEC Reliance with Duple Midland Donington coach body, at Anniesland Cross to the west side of Glasgow en-route for Ardrishaig in Argyll. When the Scottish Bus Group absorbed MacBrayne's routes in 1970, this route passed to Western SMT but all the Reliances went to Highland Omnibuses. *Iain MacGregor*

Opposite, top At the western end of its territory, Scottish Omnibuses HH552 (OWS 552) was one of 20 Leyland Titan PD2/20s with 56-seat Park Royal lowbridge bodies new in February and March 1957 to help provide additional services after Glasgow Corporation withdrew its tram services to Coatbridge and Airdrie the previous November. They were the only postwar Titans the company bought new and it is believed that the chassis were diverted from an Edinburgh Corporation order; certainly some had chassis numbers in the same series. This 1958 photograph shows a gleaming machine bound for Drumpark, in Coatbridge, with the traditional 'SMT Edinburgh' diamond fleetname. The location is the long vanished Cunningham Street, a city centre terminus over the wall from Alexander's Dundas Street bus station where the roof of a blue single-decker is visible. *Geoffrey Morant*

Opposite, lower Besides the PD2s, Park Royal supplied Scottish Omnibuses with 97 bodies on AEC Reliances and Monocoaches between 1954 and 1959. This September 1969 photograph is of one of the 1959 delivery, B690 (SWS 690), in the by then universal Eastern Scottish livery. Along with an Eastern Scottish Bristol Lodekka and several Alexander (Midland) double-deckers, it is in the overspill parking area at Glasgow's Buchanan Street bus station, next to warehousing from the once huge railway goods station there. The Midland Fleetline directly behind is one of 25 new in 1967 in an experimental livery with cream window surrounds and roof. Today's Buchanan Bus Station was built on this site, opening in 1976. *Omnibus Society/Roy Marshall*

Western SMT operated into Glasgow from the south from Renfrewshire and Ayrshire and also became the dominant operator in Paisley from 1950/51 following its acquisition of Young's Bus Service and its Paisley & District subsidiary, until then the largest independent in Scotland. The Young's fleet included 12 of these Northern Counties-bodied Leyland Titan PD2/1s new in 1948, which remained with Western until 1967. Leading a pair of them away from one of this textiles town's mill buildings is JD2167 (XS 6419). Western added 2,000 to the Young's fleet numbers and a new Daimler Fleetline soon assumed the identity of 2167 later in 1967. The prefix letters indicate depot (in this case J for Johnstone) and type (D for Leyland double-deck). *Omnibus Society/Roy Marshall*

In 1960, Western SMT bought 23 Leyland Titan PD3/3s with 67-seat lowbridge bodies by Burlingham, the Blackpool coachbuilder acquired that year by Duple. As is evident on MD1588 (OCS 122), they blended Northern Counties glazing within a more rounded body profile. They were among the last double-deckers built by Burlingham. An Alexander-bodied Daimler Fleetline is following along Clyde Street, Glasgow. *Omnibus Society/Roy Marshall*

Western SMT's prototype Alexander-bodied Albion Lowlander MN1703 (TCS 151), new in 1961, on one of the routes serving leafy suburbs in Renfrewshire. Production Lowlanders had a modified front windscreen arrangement to accommodate the Scottish Bus Group's triangular destination displays with numbers above the destination. *Campbell Sayers*

Western was the first Scottish Bus Group company to order rear-engined double-deckers, starting with 55 lowheight Alexander-bodied Daimler Fleetlines in 1965. This 1970s view shows one of that batch, JR1977 (BCS 960C), at Renfrew Ferry. The light blue structure on the right is part of a disused vehicular ferry from the Govan-Whiteinch crossing closed after the Clyde Tunnel opened in 1963. Its deck raised or lowered within the superstructure to take account of tide levels. *Omnibus Society/Peter Henson*

The Glasgow and Paisley Independents

Lowland Motorways, in which the Glasgow and Preston dealer Millburn Motors had an interest, built up a network of routes serving the East End of Glasgow before selling out to Scottish Omnibuses in January 1958. Among the last additions to the fleet were seven Cravens-bodied AEC Regent IIIs from London Transport of which 38 (JXC 181) had been RT1422 in London. *Omnibus Society/Roy Marshall*

Cunningham's Bus Service was one of the main operators on the busy service between Paisley and Renfrew Ferry, which makes the short crossing to Yoker on the Glasgow side of the River Clyde. Operated between 1956 and 1958 was 16 (DGB 413), one of five Weymann-bodied AEC Regents acquired from Glasgow Corporation, to whom they were new in 1940. *Geoffrey Morant*

The histories of these three Cunningham's double-deckers date this photograph to 1955. DLU 308 and DLU 137 are 1937 ex-London Transport STL-class AEC Regents, which were STL1916 and STL2138 respectively in London. BGA 98 on the right still wears the green and black of Daniel Ferguson of Renfrew, whose share of the Paisley-Renfrew Ferry route Cunningham's acquired in July 1954. This was one of Glasgow Corporation's first Daimlers, from a batch of 25 Weymann-bodied COG6s delivered in 1937 and withdrawn in 1950/51. Ferguson bought six of them, selling three to Cunningham's, which already had another of the same batch. BGA 98 was the last in service, in December 1955. *Geoffrey Morant*

Cunningham's 51 (HCS 998), a lowbridge Northern Counties-bodied Leyland Titan PD2/20 new to Western SMT in 1956 and acquired in 1970, at the Renfrew Ferry with the chain-driven ferry behind. Cunningham's sold out to Western in August 1979. *Omnibus Society/ Peter Henson*

Cunningham's first new double-decker, 47 (EXS 228F), arrived in September 1967. This Alexander-bodied Leyland Atlantean PDR1/1 with Leyland O.680 engine and air pedestal gearshift was an extra in a large batch being built for Glasgow Corporation, identical in practically every respect — green interior trim included — apart from the two-line destination display set to show both ends of the Ferry route. This is Moss Street, the setting down point behind Gilmour Street railway station in Paisley. *Omnibus Society/Harry Hay*

Paton Bros of Renfrew shared operation of the Paisley-Renfrew Ferry route with Cunningham's. The application of its blue and cream livery was sometimes influenced by the style of its vehicles' previous owners. A case in point was a trio of Weymann Orion-bodied Leyland Titan PD2/20s new to St Helens Corporation in 1956 and acquired in 1969. On these, the blue replaced St Helens red and white covered the municipal's cream. This is FDJ 832 on the Ferry Road, identified as No.2 in a short-lived series that allocated the lowest numbered buses to the Ferry route. *Omnibus Society/ Harry Hay*

Paton's acquired five of Edinburgh's rebuilt all-Leyland Titan PD2/12s in the latter part of 1970, when they were 18 years old, operating them for about a year on the Paisley-Renfrew Ferry route that it shared with Cunningham's. Longest lived of the quintet was KFS 944, formerly Edinburgh 253, which was withdrawn at the end of 1971. *Omnibus Society/Peter Henson*

Paton's was the first of the Paisley independents to introduce one-man operation, initially on the Govan Cross route. FYS 698 was one of four ex-Glasgow Corporation Leyland Royal Tiger Worldmasters acquired in 1970 and kept for around a year. All four were exported to Australia where the other three were rebodied. Paton's sold out to Western SMT at the same time as Cunningham's. *Omnibus Society/Harry Hay*

Graham's of Paisley and Paton Bros of Renfrew both operated services connecting Paisley by different routes with Govan Cross in what was the heart of Glasgow's shipbuilding industry. The two operators' contrasting fleets are apparent in this view in Govan a few years before the tenement housing was bulldozed for redevelopment. Graham's 60 (GXS 621), new in 1963, was the first of 13 Alexander-bodied Daimler Fleetlines bought new over the next 10 years. The blue and cream Paton's double-decker is a Weymann-bodied Leyland Titan PD2/4 new to Bury Corporation in 1950 and acquired in 1964. *Geoffrey Morant*

The last new half cab double-decker for Graham's was Strachans-bodied Guy Arab IV 56 (FXS 601), which was built in 1962 but did not enter service until January 1964. Strachans exhibited it at the September 1962 Commercial Motor Show at Earls Court in London and it was issued with this Paisley registration mark the following month. It then failed its tilt test and underwent modifications, including reducing the upper saloon seating capacity by four. It had the style of bonnet that Guy developed initially for buses supplied to Johannesburg and remained with Graham's until 1977. *Geoffrey Morant*

Graham's continued to buy secondhand Guy Arab IVs until 1971, keeping the last of them until 1975. Northern Counties-bodied 77 (TTE 146), new in 1954 to Lancashire United, was the first of five consecutively registered 59-seaters purchased in 1967/68. It was operated until 1971 and photographed in Paisley town centre in June 1968. Graham's ceased trading in April 1990. *Omnibus Society/Roy Marshall*

McGill's of Barrhead connected its home town with Paisley and, at certain times, Renfrew Ferry where this photograph was taken of DHS172, one of a pair of all-Leyland Titan PD1s new in 1947 and kept until 1965. It discontinued the application of maroon paint, confined latterly to bus roofs, in 1964. *Jim Thomson*

These three double-deckers were among the most remarkable in the McGill's fleet. They were Weymann-bodied AEC Regents new to Sheffield Corporation in 1936. McGill's acquired them in 1948 and 1949, rebuilding them at a later date and keeping them until 1960/61. BWJ 734 and CWJ 404 were fitted with Leyland-style radiators embossed with a McGill's badge, while CWJ 405 on the left got Barrhead's answer to the 'New Look' fronts that came into fashion in the early 1950s, with concealed radiator and boxed nearside mudguard and wing. *Jim Thomson*

McGill's received four Park Royal-bodied Guy Arab II utility double-deckers in 1944/45 and had them rebodied by Massey in 1955. This 1958 view shows CHS 271, new in August 1944 and the last survivor of the quartet, as it finally departed for scrap in 1972. *Geoffrey Morant*

McGill's did not operate into Glasgow until the 1980s when it won a lengthy battle to establish a new service. Until 1977, it operated its bus routes exclusively with double-deckers. FHS 181K was one of two lowheight Alexander-bodied Daimler Fleetlines new in 1971, shown here operating a Paisley-Barrhead service. *Omnibus Society/Roy Marshall*

Smith's of Barrhead, owned by the Scottish Cooperative Wholesale Society from 1947 until Western SMT took over its routes in 1968, ran to Paisley and the Glasgow suburb of South Nitshill. MGB 623, a 1954 Leyland Titan PD2/12 with one of the last lowbridge bodies built by Leyland Motors, approaches a stop in Paisley. Because SCWS had its head office in Glasgow, Smith's buses were registered in the city rather than Renfrewshire. *Omnibus Society/Roy Marshall*

Garner's Buses operated into Paisley from its home village of Bridge of Weir until December 1968, when it gave this up along with another stage carriage route in Renfrewshire after its garage was lost to redevelopment. Preparing to leave the Paisley terminus in 1965 is HAV 385, a 1952 all-Leyland Royal Tiger PSU1/13 bus new to Simpson's of Rosehearty and operated by Garner's from 1960 to 1967. Paisley coach operator Matthew Pattison provided a replacement service from 1969 to 1973, when Graham's took over. A low railway bridge dictated the use of single-deckers. *Omnibus Society/Roy Marshall*

Aberdeen Independents

Three independents operated into Aberdeen until the mid-1960s. Strachan's Deeside Omnibus Service was based in Ballater and served the north and south Deeside routes from Braemar and Ballater until Alexander (Northern) bought the business in May 1965. Nearest the camera in Bon Accord Street is 20 (DSA 100), a Roberts-bodied Foden PVSC6. Alongside is Park Royal-bodied Daimler COG5 number 6 (DHP 206), new to Coventry Corporation in 1938, acquired in 1950 and withdrawn in 1962. SMT Sales & Service was the Vauxhall and Bedford dealership business originally in common ownership with what became the Scottish Bus Group. *Alan B Cross*

Simpson's of Rosehearty operated around the Fraserburgh area and between the Buchan communities and Aberdeen. Among vehicles operated on its local routes at the beginning of the 1960s was ARG 82, one of several prewar ex-Aberdeen Corporation Daimler COG6s acquired at that time. It had bodywork by Walker's of Aberdeen, was new in 1939 and ran with Simpson's from 1961 to 1963. Simpson's sold out to Alexander (Northern) in December 1966. *Omnibus Society/Roy Marshall*

The third of the Aberdeenshire independents was Burnett's of Mintlaw, which Northern acquired in January 1967. Among the vehicles it acquired was PWL 412, an ex-City of Oxford AEC Regent III with lowbridge Weymann body, which remained with Northern for four years. *Omnibus Society/ Roy Marshall*

Burnett's bought two of these Walker-bodied Daimler COG6s from Aberdeen Corporation in January 1961. No 9 (RG 8121) was new to Aberdeen in May 1938 as its 121. Alongside is No 6 (CSA 145) an Albion Valkyrie new in 1946. *Omnibus Society/Roy Marshall*

Dundee and Perth Independents

Greyhound of Arbroath, the Scottish offshoot of a business founded in Sheffield by a member of the Alexander family, operated a stage service into Dundee, worked here by 71 (GFM 887), an ECW-bodied Bristol L6A new to Crosville and acquired from Thames Valley in 1965.
Omnibus Society/Roy Marshall

The Perthshire independent, A & C McLennan of Spittalfield, operated into Perth and also between Perth, Errol and Dundee where its terminus was next to the Dundee Corporation bus station in Dock Street. By the time this picture was taken in 1976, the bus station had gone and Tayside Regional Council's offices were rising in its place; the council was abolished 20 years later and the offices have been torn down. Operating the Errol route that day was GTS 397, a Duple Britannia-bodied AEC Reliance coach new to Watson's Tours of Dundee in 1957, acquired by McLennan's in 1968 and withdrawn in 1979. McLennan's was acquired by Stagecoach in 1985.
Alan Millar

Streamers pour from McLennan's DRS 363, an ex-Aberdeen 1951 Daimler CVG6 with 1960 Alexander bodywork, as it sets out from Mill Street, Perth on what appears to be a Sunday school outing. McLennan's bought three of these rebodied buses from Greyhound of Arbroath in 1971, fitting platform doors and operating them until 1976, the year this picture was taken. They operated regularly on the Perth-Stanley service. *Geoffrey Morant*

Between 1948 and 1963, McLennan's built 20 new single-deck bodies for its own use and at least five for other Scottish operators. The only example on a mid-underfloor engined chassis was this one on EES 468, a Leyland Royal Tiger PSU1/15 new in 1952 with 43 coach seats. It survived in the fleet until 1973 when it was traded in against a Plaxton-boded Ford R1114, which was also of note as being the last new vehicle McLennan's bought in its 40-year existence. *Omnibus Society/Roy Marshall*

Between 1958 and 1965, McLennan's bought 11 former London Transport RTL-class Leyland Titan PD2s, fitting their Park Royal bodies with platform doors and keeping the last of them until 1976. The former RTL40 (JXN 363) arrived in July 1958 and was withdrawn in October 1971. This picture shows it at the firm's garage at Spittalfield in June 1969. *Omnibus Society/ Harry Hay*

Day tours, provided mainly by Scottish Bus Group companies but also by some independents, operated from all of the cities in summer months. An enduring sight alongside the Dundee Corporation buses at Dock Street bus station was Fyffe's Tours ATS 689, a Duple Vista-bodied Bedford OB supplied new in 1949 and operated on daily excursions well into the 1970s. The lettering on the side may boast trips from Lands End to John O'Groats and the destination blind reads Scottish Highlands, but by the time this picture was taken in 1973 the destinations were more local. Legend had it that the only mystery involved in Fyffe's mystery tours was whether they began or ended by crossing the Tay Road Bridge; the same legend had it that the regulars wanted no more of a surprise. This coach survives in preservation. *Omnibus Society/Roy Marshall*